MISSION: BLACK LIST #1

MISSION:
BLACK LIST #1

**THE INSIDE STORY OF THE
SEARCH FOR SADDAM HUSSEIN—
AS TOLD BY THE SOLDIER
WHO MASTERMINDED HIS CAPTURE**

ERIC MADDOX WITH DAVIN SEAY

HARPER

An Imprint of HarperCollinsPublishers
www.harpercollins.com

FIRST EDITION

Designed by William Ruoto

Library of Congress Cataloging-in-Publication Data is available upon request.

ISBN: 978-0-06-171447-4

08 09 10 11 12   OV/RRD   10 9 8 7 6 5 4 3 2 1

To all of those who have served, fought, and sacrificed,
and to all those who yearn for a seat at the bar

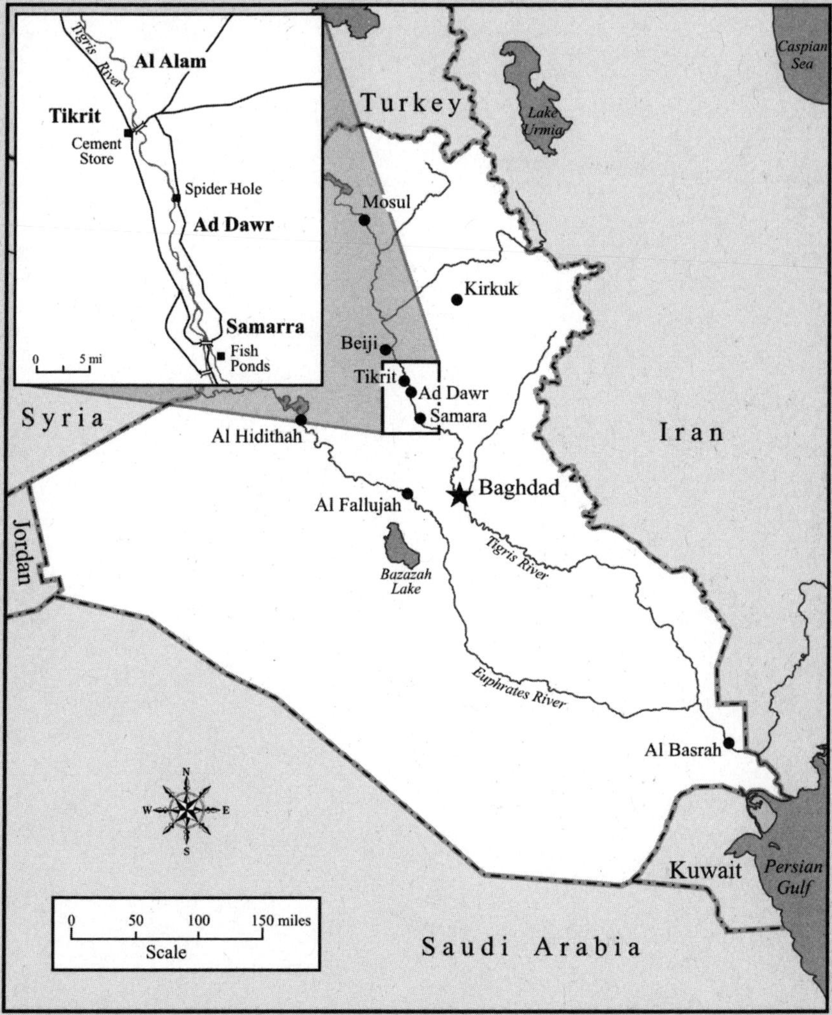

Tigris River
Al Alam
Tikrit
Cement Store
Spider Hole
Ad Dawr
Samarra
Fish Ponds
0 5 mi
Caspian Sea
Turkey
Lake Urmia
Mosul
Kirkuk
Beiji
Tikrit
Ad Dawr
Samara
Syria
Al Hidithah
Iran
Baghdad
Al Fallujah
Jordan
Bazazah Lake
Tigris River
Euphrates River
Al Basrah
N
W
E
S
Kuwait
Persian Gulf
0 50 100 150 miles
Scale
Saudi Arabia

CONTENTS

MISSION: BLACK LIST #1

PROLOGUE

1400 15DEC2003

A cold blast of December air hit me as I made my way down the connecting corridor into the busy terminal of Heathrow Airport. Holiday travelers, hurrying home for Christmas, surrounded me on every side. The crowded airport seemed like a surreal place, safe and clean and worlds away from the war I had been fighting. Despite the noise, all I could hear was the beating of my heart as I thought back to the place I'd just left. It was a whole other reality, one that changed forever not just who I was, but the world I was about to reenter.

I wanted that dreamlike feeling to last, that inward sense of satisfaction that I had done my job and completed my mission. But my focus right then was on another mission: to find coming-home gifts for my two boys, Joe and Eric Marshall. In my travels, I always made a point of bringing back souvenirs for my young sons. There were no gift stores where I'd spent the last five months, so something quick and easy from the London airport would have to do. But the Tony Blair bobble heads and Big Ben shot glasses in the gift store probably weren't going to do the trick. As I looked around for something more suitable, a television in an airport pub across the way caught my eye.

I wasn't the only one. A small crowd began to gather, watching the breaking news report. On screen, a man walked up to a podium in a room filled with cameras and reporters. His name appeared as he cleared his throat and leaned into the microphones: Ambassador L. Paul Bremer, the head of the Coalition Provisional Authority in Iraq.

The noise of the airport seemed to die down as we strained to hear what he would say. It was as if we somehow already knew that this was one of those events we would always remember, a key moment in history.

"Ladies and gentlemen," Bremer said. "We got him."

There were probably only a handful of people in the world watching at that moment who didn't know what Bremer was talking about. But his next words left no doubt. "Saddam Hussein was captured Saturday, December thirteenth, at eight-thirty P.M. local time in a cellar in the town of Ad Dawr, which is some fifteen kilometers south of Tikrit."

The sound of cheering in the pressroom blended into the buzz of the crowd around me, a mix of surprise and skepticism. An old man at the bar turned to his friend and said, "They had him the whole time. Bush is bringing him out now just to win the bloody election."

I closed my eyes and smiled as the two drinking buddies agreed that the capture of the most wanted man in the world was nothing more than a political stunt. The truth was, there was only one person at that bar, in that airport, or anywhere else for that matter, who knew the real story of Saddam Hussein's capture.

I was that person.

An hour later, I was still thinking about that chatter in the pub as I settled into my seat for the long flight home. Maybe the real story of the hunt for Saddam would never be known. But if it ever *was* told, where would it begin? As we lifted into the murky London sky, I looked down on the city below. I remembered another landscape I'd once flown over, a long way from these peaceful rows of suburban houses. It seemed as good a place as any to start.

CHAPTER 1

NIGHT RIDE

2200 28JUL2003

We came in low, a hundred feet over the desert under the cover of night. The tiny two-man OH-58 scout helicopter was moving at eighty miles an hour, skimming over the farms and small villages. But I wasn't noticing the view. I was too busy hanging on for dear life, tethered to the chopper and stuffed into a space behind the pilot so small that my legs dangled in midair. Beside me was my kit, packed, as I'd been ordered, with enough gear for two days.

It had been four days since I first arrived in Iraq, landing at the military base at Baghdad International Airport (BIAP) along with my friend and fellow interrogator, Lee. We had been assigned together in the Defense Intelligence Agency for almost two years, and in that time Lee had earned a reputation as a top-notch interrogator. But, for me, this was the first real shot I'd have at doing the job I signed up for back in 1999. Since then I'd never had the chance to even question a prisoner. This time I was determined to make the most of the opportunity and from almost the moment I landed, I got to work interrogating the detainees in the prison built in an airport hangar on the base.

I'd kept it up day and night since then, grabbing a meal or a few hours' sleep between sessions. After a few days, some of the other interrogators advised me to pace myself. It was easy to burn out in this job. But I didn't want to hear that. Nobody knew when this war might get shut down. Until that happened, I wanted to get in as much interrogation experience as I could.

But I was also beginning to realize that the prisoners I was questioning were sometimes nothing more than frightened and confused civilians, not the bad guys we were looking for.

"Bad guys" was the term we used for anyone we were going after. They could be insurgents, former members of Saddam's regime, or just troublemakers who crossed our path at the wrong time but to us, they were "bad guys." There were a lot of them that summer. The invasion of Iraq had begun back in March and enough time had passed for the opposition to begin to organize itself. Former Baathists and regime officials; army officers; foreign fighters and jihadists: we faced a wide variety of enemies.

As a result our intelligence gathering efforts were ramped up. I was part of a group of case officers, analysts, and interrogators from various agencies and military branches. We had one overall mission: to gather actionable intelligence on the identities, influence, and whereabouts of the insurgents. It was a steep learning curve.

I began to wonder whether our efforts were stalling for a lack of good information. Most of our intelligence was provided by paid informants, who obviously had an incentive to give us leads, whether or not they were solid. Maybe there was a better way to get at what we needed to know.

Within twenty-four hours of our arrival Lee and I were asked if we'd be willing to serve as interrogators on "hits," the raids that were conducted in Baghdad to search for High Value Targets and round up suspected insurgents. Neither one of us had been beyond the perimeter of the airport. We were eager, both for the opportunity to be useful, and for a chance to get "outside the wire" for the first time. Since Lee was senior to me, he would obviously be the first to go, but he promised me that I would get the next available mission.

The night of the hit, I could see that he was excited and even a little nervous, although he did his best not to show it. I could understand why. It was dangerous work. But forever after he'd be able to say he was part of a wartime raid in hostile territory.

But with only minutes to go before the hit was launched, it was abruptly canceled. Disappointed, Lee headed back to his quarters.

"Does that count?" I asked him, half joking.

He gave me a look. "No," he said, then shrugged. "I'm turning in. If something comes up in the next few hours, it's yours."

Something did. Later that evening, while he was still in the rack, a soldier came looking for him. "He's asleep," I told him. "What's up?"

"They're looking for an interrogator to go to Tikrit."

My heart skipped a beat. "What's going on?"

"They captured a bodyguard up there," he explained. "Drunk off his ass, but he might know something."

"So what do I need to do?"

"Are you cleared to go?" he asked skeptically.

"Yeah," I replied. "I'm actually on standby for anything that comes up."

"Pack enough for a couple of days," he told me. "Grab your weapon. The chopper's waiting."

★ ★ ★

My lack of sleep over the last few days was beginning to catch up with me as we took the ninety-minute flight to Tikrit. But every time I started to doze off, I could feel myself slipping out of that metal mosquito and snapped back awake.

We finally set down on a small landing pad. Numb from the rotor vibrations and deep fatigue, I fumbled to unlatch myself from the tether. From out of the shadows a big, hulking guy with a handlebar mustache appeared and without waiting for an invitation, pulled me from the chopper.

"You the interrogator?" he asked.

I nodded and stumbled after him to a waiting Humvee. I assumed that I was in Tikrit, but had no way of knowing. I could barely make out the outlines of the military compound in the darkness and only later found out that I had landed at Camp Ironhorse, headquarters of the 4th Infantry Division, responsible for Tikrit and the northern section of the Sunni Triangle. After a few minutes we passed through a checkpoint and continued into the driveway of an imposing marble mansion.

I would learn a lot about Tikrit in the days that followed. As the hometown of Saddam Hussein, it was full of the palaces, estates, and farms of the ruling elite, mostly members of Saddam's extended family and the allies of his clan. The mansion where we had arrived had actually been a vacation getaway for Saddam's wife.

The place had a huge two-story front with a balcony that ran around its upper floor. I followed my guide through the wide front door and into the spacious reception hall, stacked high with crates of ammunition and an impressive array of weaponry. The only remnants of the former occupants were some sofas and sideboards and a few pictures of Saddam still hanging on the wall. We headed up a wide sweeping stairway to the second floor and down a long dim corridor and into a brightly lit room. A group of soldiers were gathered around a map, talking in low tones. It was only later that I realized I had walked into the midst of an Operations Order. These men were planning a mission.

Their intense concentration shifted from the map to me as we entered. The driver made the introductions, first to Jack, a major who was the commanding officer of the small elite task force headquartered at the mansion. They were, I knew, superbly trained and equipped and tasked with some of the most danger-ous and difficult missions of the war. True to their reputation, as I would come to discover, they didn't have much use for anyone who wasn't part of their world. They were never rude or arro-gant, but because they were the best of the best, they didn't want to have to deal with anyone who wasn't.

That attitude was summed up by the cool appraisal I got from Matt, the second in command. At six feet two inches and two hundred twenty pounds, with shoulders like bowling balls, Matt made an immediate impression. And the look he gave me that night made it clear he had no use for straphangers. In Air-borne terminology, a straphanger is a paratrooper who just goes along for the ride, trying to log the required number of jumps. Until I could prove otherwise, I was a straphanger.

"Don't I know you from somewhere?" he asked, still look-ing me up and down.

I swallowed hard. I would have remembered meeting this dude, but maybe I'd pissed him off in a bar somewhere or, worse, hit on his girlfriend back in the States. "I don't think so," I muttered and tried to change the subject. "I was told you needed an interrogator."

A third member of the team, a wiry redhead, stepped forward and introduced himself as Jeff. "We got a couple of detainees we think are Saddam bodyguards," he explained in a deep Texas accent. "One of them is too drunk to talk but the other might actually know something."

"I'm here to talk to anyone you want me to."

"That's good," Jack cut in. "Because before you start, we've got something else we need you to do."

"Anything."

"We're getting ready to go on a raid," he explained, nodding at the map in front of them. "We'd like you to come along."

* * *

It was close to midnight when Jeff, Jack, and Matt gave me a quick rundown on the raid. We would be following up a lead from a low-level source claiming that one of Saddam's old bodyguards was in a farmhouse on the outskirts of town. He was supposed to be leaving that morning for Syria to meet Saddam. My job was to find out where that meeting would take place.

After the briefing, they sent me downstairs, where a half dozen other soldiers were methodically preparing for the mission. With zero idea what to take on a hit, I started rummaging through the baggage I had brought with me from Baghdad.

"Got everything you need?" Matt asked, coming up behind me.

"Should I, uh, take my rifle?" I must have looked as dumb as I felt.

"Yeah," he replied dryly. "A weapon is a good idea."

"And how about my helmet?"

"Always useful," he agreed. Whatever impression he had of me upstairs, I wasn't doing much to improve it. I decided not to ask any more questions.

Jeff arrived to introduce me to my interpreter, or "terp" as they're called. His name was Jared, and he looked to me as if going on this raid was the last thing he wanted to be doing.

I'd already had some experience with terps back in Baghdad. They were mostly Iraqi-Americans who had been contracted by the military for their language skills. A lot of them had the attitude that they knew everything and the interrogator knew nothing. In my case, that was actually true. If you asked what they thought was a stupid question, they'd roll their eyes and start asking their own. If you got a rambling answer from a prisoner they'd tell you he didn't know anything and leave it at that. They were definitely on our team, but, in most cases, that didn't make working with them any easier.

Jared surely wasn't interested in making things easier. It wasn't until Jeff pulled me aside that I found out why. The terp was shipping out the next day, he told me. This would be his last mission.

"I appreciate your helping me out tonight, Jared," I said as we sat together lacing our boots. "I've been down in Baghdad this whole time. What's the target set here in Tikrit?" The "target set" was the known list of bad guys the team was looking for in Tikrit. I was determined to get as much information as I could, regardless of how foolish it made me look. And I must have looked pretty foolish, considering the fed-up expression on

Jared's face. He continued silently lacing his boots as I tried another approach. "I guess you've been here awhile," I said. "Any tips for a newcomer?"

That caught his interest. Now I wasn't just asking for information; I was asking for his opinion. "Focus on Saddam's bodyguards," he said while around us the preparations for the raid continued. "They are all relatives of Saddam and they are all from Tikrit." He looked at me. "I have a list. Alphabetical. With all their sub-tribes. I write down if they are killed, captured, or unknown. Over two hundred names."

"No shit. Can I see it?"

"It's all on the computer, but you can have my copy." He rummaged in his pack and pulled out several sheets of paper filled with single-spaced columns.

I took a quick look at his handiwork, immediately noting the "Unknown" status written alongside most of the names. "Wow," I said. "How did you put all this together?"

His bored attitude quickly disappeared. He obviously took a lot of pride in his accomplishment. "Over the last few months I kept running across bodyguards and their family members," he told me. "So I made the list. For example, tonight the bodyguard we are going after is an Al-Muslit. That's one of the big tribes loyal to Saddam." He pointed to a section of about forty Al-Muslits on his list.

"Anyone I should be paying special attention to?" I pressed. I could tell he appreciated my interest in his work. I had his attention now. I also had the feeling that what he was telling me might prove very useful.

He tapped his finger next to another name on the list. "Al-Haddoushi," he said. "Especially Muhammad Al-Haddoushi. He was very close to Saddam." He leaned forward. " They may still be in contact."

There was something else I needed to know. "Why did you focus on the bodyguards?" I asked Jared.

"Look," he said, as if he was explaining it to a kid, "there's attacks going on all the time in Tikrit. IEDs, RPGs, ambushes. Somebody has to be doing it. I think these bodyguards might have some answers."

"So you're an interrogator?"

He shook his head, and then nodded at the men around us, getting ready for the raid. "These guys do their own interrogating," he explained. "I just translate. But when they're done, they sometimes let me ask questions about my list. After that, we ship the prisoners down to Baghdad, to the BIAP jail. I guess they get interrogated down there."

I knew better. There were so many detainees at the airport compound that most of the them were just being stored until someone could figure out what to do with them. Detainees brought from Tikrit and elsewhere were not a high priority. But the information the terp was providing had given me an idea. After five days in Baghdad, interrogating mostly low-level prisoners, I didn't feel as if I'd accomplished a lot. Maybe I'd be of more use in Tikrit. And maybe there was something to Jared's bodyguard theory.

"You think they could use a full-time interrogator up here?" I asked.

"Not really. We've been able to handle it so far."

That wasn't the answer I was looking for, so I came at it from another direction. "Where do you guys get your intelligence?" I asked.

Over the next few minutes, Jared gave me a rundown on the insurgency situation in Tikrit. It was the 4th Infantry Division, he told me, which had initially developed informant sources in the area and passed along whatever information they gleaned to the task force. They were kept pretty busy at first, hunting down the High Value Targets that were still clustered in Saddam's hometown. But it wasn't long before that well had run dry. The way the terp saw it, the only reason they were still in the area was because of Izzat Ibrahim Al-Duri.

"Who's that?" I asked, once again showing my ignorance.

"He's Black List number six," Jared told me. "You know, from the deck of cards?"

That part I got. The DOD had put together a pack of playing cards at the beginning of the war. On the face of the cards were the fifty-five most wanted men in Iraq: the Black List. Saddam was Black List #1, the Ace of Spades. His sons, Uday and Qusay were BLs #2 and #3. They'd already been accounted for, killed in a bloody shoot-out in Mosul the day before I arrived in Baghdad. BL #4 was the presidential secretary, Hamid Mahmud, while #5 on the list was the notorious Chemical Ali. As BL #6, Al-Duri, the King of Clubs, was a top military adviser to Saddam and a prime suspect in the insurgent activities around Tikrit. There were fifty-two in all. Along with the three Jokers that made it fifty-five.

The deck of cards was part of a major effort to take the hunt for Saddam and his cronies nationwide. There was no question that finding him was a top priority. Ground troops, Special Operations Forces, and intelligence operatives had scoured the country in the months after the invasion. Every person on the deck was a High Value Target for the U.S. military. But there was only one Ace of Spades. I never heard anyone say it, but we would have gladly traded every wanted man on the entire deck of cards for Saddam.

"We're pretty sure Al-Duri is still around here somewhere,"

Jared told me. "If we can find Al-Duri, he might lead us to Saddam."

I wanted to ask another question. I wanted to ask a lot of other questions. But Jared's information dump was over. The team was ready, locked, and loaded. The hit was about to happen.

CHAPTER 2

OUTSIDE THE WIRE

0045 29JUL2003

A total of eight of us would go on tonight's raid. Aside from Jared and me, there were six shooters from the task force, including a guy who introduced himself to me as Carl. He'd been given the chore of keeping an eye on me during the operation.

"Stick close," he said. "We'll be attached to a platoon from Fourth ID. Our job is strictly SSE." He saw the puzzled expression on my face. "Sensitive Site Exploitation," he patiently explained. "Fourth ID will lock down the location. Then we'll go in for a search and interrogate whoever we find."

"Al-Muslit." I nodded, remembering what Jared had told me.

"That's the plan," he replied, but something in his voice told me that a hit doesn't always go according to plan. I followed him out to the rear of the mansion where two top-of-the-line Mercedes sedans were parked. I found out later that the luxury ride I was in had previously been driven by two teenage nieces of Saddam's, the daughters of his half brother Barzan. Barzan was one of the most wanted men in Iraq, the Five of Clubs in the deck of High Value Targets; his house had been raided shortly before my arrival. The team had been using the girls' car ever since.

It was after one A.M. when Jared and I climbed into the backseat of one of the Mercedes, with Carl at the wheel and another shooter, named Sam, riding shotgun. The other four members of the team were in the car in front of us. We peeled out and headed off at top speed to link up with the 4th ID platoon at their camp near Beiji, a village just north of Tikrit.

Whatever lingering fatigue I had evaporated in a rush of adrenaline. Traveling between the compound and the 4th ID outpost, we were in enemy territory, subject to RPGs, sniper fire and anything else they could throw at us. And, since there was a nine P.M. curfew in place, anyone on the road at that hour had to be an American. We needed to get where we were going fast, and within minutes were rocketing through clouds of dust at a hundred miles an hour.

As we skidded into the last curve that would take us down a mile-long straightaway to Beiji, the darkness around us suddenly erupted in deafening chaos. The driver lurched violently to avoid the gunfire and it felt like we were trapped inside a rolling steel drum as he swerved. From the flashes of light and the thudding noise, I knew that a fifty-caliber machine gun had opened up on us. I also knew that, with a gun as big as a fifty-cal, it's hard to miss.

The car in front of us had disappeared into the dust as Carl slammed on the brakes and we went into a long slide. "Oh fuck!" someone said, as Carl threw open the door and jumped out.

"Secure the vehicle!" he shouted to Sam as he ran into the darkness, yelling, "USA! USA!"

As quickly as it had started, the incoming fire was over and the three of us sat in silence waiting for what would happen next. I remember thinking nothing, my mind still reeling from the reality of getting shot at, my pulse hammering in my ears. So this was what it was like outside the wire.

After what seemed an eternity, Carl reappeared in the beams of the headlights. He got back in the driver's seat, gripping the steering wheel and trying to catch his breath.

"What happened, man?" asked Sam.

"The guard up ahead didn't get word we were coming through," Carl said, starting the car again and pulling back onto the road. "He said we fired first. I guess that's the standard line when you light up your own guys. Luckily he couldn't shoot straight."

"What about the others?"

"They're okay. Let's just get linked up and we'll figure out what went wrong later." He turned to the backseat. "You all right?"

"No problem," I said as casually as possible. The last thing Carl needed was some cherry interrogator freaking out on him. He had other things to think about. So did I. I couldn't remember if I had packed an extra pair of underwear, but the ones I was wearing were ruined for sure. I'd never been in a friendly fire incident before and I found myself wondering who'd come up with that expression. Friendly or not, a fifty-caliber round is still going to kill you.

★ ★ ★

The 4th ID platoon that was waiting for us at the Beiji camp was actually more the size of a full company. I would later discover that this was how they handled most of their operations, with more manpower than was really called for. As we traded our Benzes for a Humvee, I got a chance to talk briefly with the intelligence officer who had developed the information for the raid. His source was a kid, he told me, who had previously turned up some weapons caches. But tonight was different. This was the informant's first big target.

The name of the bodyguard we were after, I found out, was Nezham Hasan Jasim Al-Muslit. It was a mouthful, like most Arabic names, made up of your grandfather's, your father's, and your given name, along with your tribal affiliation. It was complicated and confusing, but it was also very useful in establishing links and interlocking alliances. Just by looking at a man's name, you could tell to whom he was related and even where his loyalties lay.

According to the informant, Nezham's loyalties were firmly with Saddam, his former boss. Nezham was supposed to be driving across the Syrian border that morning. Maybe he was going there to meet with Saddam. I wanted to know where the kid had gotten such valuable intelligence, but it didn't seem like my place to ask. So I climbed in the Humvee with the rest of the team and we drove up the road as Carl explained what was about to happen.

"We're going to hang back and let them do the raid. Then we'll search the place." He turned to me. "You talk to whoever's in there and let me know what you find out."

The Humvee pulled off the road and the team dismounted to set up a security perimeter. Jared and I stayed close to the vehicle and for about thirty seconds there was nothing to listen to but the buzz of insects. It was only when I heard the unmistakable sound of a door being broken down that I realized how close to the house we actually were.

Uncomfortably close. Almost immediately an AK-47 started chattering, dumping a thirty-round clip. It had to be an insurgent; coalition forces didn't use that weapon. There was some random yelling, followed by a few piercing screams. Then, once again, silence. After five tense minutes, the radio crackled to life. We'd gotten word to move up.

The dusty yard was full of 4th ID soldiers posted around a typical Iraqi farmhouse, mud brick and cinderblock built low to the ground. As we approached the front door, hanging off its hinges, Carl signaled for one of the shooters to accompany me inside. "This is Superfly," he told me. I figured that since Superfly had been stuck babysitting me; he was probably one of the junior members of the team. Jared joined us.

In a large room with a low ceiling, a man was sitting on the floor. Standing over him were a couple of 4th ID guards.

"Here's your guy," one of them said as we entered.

The prisoner's hands were cuffed behind his back and a heavy blindfold covered his eyes. His shirt was drenched in blood and I could see it running down his jaw and neck.

"Is he shot?" I asked.

"No," replied the other guard. I wondered if he noticed how pale I'd turned. "Lucky for him we just butt stroked him. He was the one that opened up on us."

"If we did the hit he'd have been dead as soon as we saw the muzzle flash," Superfly muttered.

I took a deep breath. "Why don't you take the blindfold off?" I suggested. I wanted to be eye to eye with this guy when I questioned him.

One of the guards obliged, pulling back the blood-soaked cloth. I'd never been very good with blood, going back to my early days in the infantry, when training accidents were not uncommon. It is something I've always tried to hide, with varying degrees of success.

This was going to be harder than most. Where the guy's left

eye should have been, there was an empty socket. I knelt down. "Are you Nezham Hasan?" I asked as Jared translated.

The prisoner, a thin, weather-beaten farmer who looked to be about fifty, shook his head.

"Who are you?"

He stuttered his name.

"Do you know Nezham Hasan?"

Shaking his head again, he looked scared, his one eye signaling panic. I leaned in closer, fighting nausea, and asked him the question again. This time he let loose with a long string of Arabic. "What's he saying?" I asked Jared.

"He says Nezham owns this place," the terp replied. "He only farms the land for him. He says he thought he was being robbed. That's why he opened fire."

"When was the last time you saw Nezham?"

"He was here four hours ago," Jared translated.

"Where is he now?" I received a look of one-eyed fear. It took a few more rounds of back and forth questioning, but I finally got him to reveal that Nezham had left earlier for his home in nearby Beiji. He went on to describe the house as having a large television antenna on the roof.

"We've been to that place before," volunteered one of the 4th ID platoon sergeants, who by this time had joined several others in watching the interrogation. "I know exactly where it is." I didn't realize it at the time, but identifying the house of a former bodyguard was, by itself, no big deal. By the time I'd arrived in Tikrit, virtually every location owned by a member of the regime had been raided at least once. The difference this time was that we might actually find one of them at home.

I passed on what I'd learned to Carl. He consulted briefly

with the 4th ID company commander. "Tell this old man he's lucky to be alive," he said to Jared afterward. "Tell him to sit here until we're all gone and not to make a move." He turned to the team. "We're going to Beiji," he said.

Twenty minutes later, the second target had been secured. It was just as the old man had described it, down to the oversize aerial on the roof. But there was no Nezham. Instead I found myself interrogating a group of five defiant teenagers, and two of them admitted to being nephews of our quarry. They hadn't seen their uncle in months, they swore. Although I knew they were lying through their teeth, I also knew we'd hit a dead end.

It was seven in the morning when we got back to the compound. The team gathered around a large table in the mansion's dining room to talk over the night's events, drinking Cokes and replaying the friendly fire incident.

At some point, someone must have shown me where to sleep. But I don't remember how I got to the cot. I don't even remember my head hitting the pillow.

CHAPTER 3

INTERROGATION 101

There was no reason to think I had any special qualifications to be an interrogator for the task force in Tikrit. From that first night of the raid, it had begun to dawn on me that getting good intelligence was going to require a different set of skills than those I'd learned in interrogation school.

That's not to say I hadn't received the best training available at the time, maybe the best in the world. In 1999 I had attended an eight-week interrogation course at the U.S. Army Intelligence Center in Fort Huachuca, Arizona. There I was taught military doctrines from Field Manual 34-52, on how to conduct effective interrogations in conformity with U.S. and international laws. I learned how to avoid getting simple yes-or-no responses by asking interrogative questions: who, what, when, where, why, what else, and what other. I was instructed in psychological approaches like Pride & Ego Up, which was meant to build up a prisoner; and Pride & Ego Down, which was meant to tear him down. I was introduced to the Geneva Convention rules prohibiting physical or mental duress, torture, or other forms of coercion to secure information.

What I didn't learn was how to actually get the job done. Most of my instructors had never interrogated a real live prisoner. There had been very few prisoners since Vietnam. The means and methods I was taught assumed I would be in a battlefield environment much like that war, or even World War II. There was no preparation for modern urban combat, where the enemy is everywhere and nowhere at the same time. I would soon find out I was going to need to start from scratch.

But as much as I had to learn, I also had innate abilities I brought to the mission. Like anyone else, I'm really smart at some things and really dumb at others. It just happens that the things I'm smart at were helpful to becoming a good interrogator. It's a certain capacity I think I was born with.

★ ★ ★

In some ways my upbringing wasn't that different from any other typical American kid. I was born in Enid, Oklahoma, and raised in the small town of Sapulpa, on the outskirts of Tulsa. I was active in my church youth group and grew up playing baseball and football. I've always loved sports especially football and even after shipping out to Iraq, I did my best to keep up with the incredible 2003–4 season the Oklahoma Sooners were having.

OU is my alma mater, where I joined a fraternity, partied hard, and tried to figure out what I wanted to do with the rest of my life. I had long since realized that, with my stature and weight—five feet nine inches and one hundred fifty-five pounds—my football career would come to a screeching halt after high school. I studied political science with some vague idea that I would go on to law school.

The fact was I had no idea what to do. After graduating, I would have the choice of staying on for a law degree or, like most white, middle-class males, I would go on to find an entry-level job in business, followed by a wife and kids and a membership at the local country club. But what I really wanted was to step out of my sheltered life for once. I needed to do something that I felt made a difference, at least in my world. I wanted to serve in the military. In the summer before my senior year I went to the U.S. Army recruiting office and signed up, postdating my enlistment date until after I graduated from OU.

Serving my country was my main goal, but I also had a close buddy who definitely motivated me. His name was Casey and we'd always had a friendly rivalry growing up in Sapulpa. Casey had joined the Army a year before I did. After that, our military careers tracked pretty closely, with Casey always being one step ahead of me. When I was in basic training, he was in Ranger School. Then, when I went to Ranger School, he went to Special Forces. It was only after he was in SF that our paths diverged. I would eventually become an interrogator and he went with his Special Forces team to Bosnia, where he was honored for saving hundreds of lives while stationed there.

It wasn't that we were in competition. I wasn't trying to catch up with him. I just looked up to him. We'd come from the same place and shared the same values. There was a bond between us that couldn't be broken even when, in April 2003, Casey died of unknown causes in his sleep. A few months later I'd find myself in Iraq, carrying the memory of my friend with me. I got to where I'd talk to him out loud about the challenges I was facing and the disappointments I was dealing with. Eventually I was even able to picture him sitting at a bar, maybe in heaven. He'd be having a beer with my grandfathers, both of whom had served with distinction in World War II. More than anything, I wanted to earn a place at that bar.

* * *

My family was similar to those of most of my friends growing up in a small town in Oklahoma, except for the slight detail that my brother and I were adopted. I was only a few days old when they brought me home from the hospital, and in the years that followed, my parents never made a secret of the fact that I was adopted.

What they couldn't provide was any information about my birth parents. Those records had all been sealed as part of the adoption procedures. But that didn't stop me from being curious and eventually that curiosity got the better of me. We would regularly drive to Enid, Oklahoma, on family visits to see my grandparents and because I knew that was my birthplace, I would stare out the car window at the people passing on the street. Any one of them could have been my mom or dad. It wasn't that I didn't love my parents, or think of them as my own. More than anything, it was that the information about who I was and where I came from was being denied me. That just made me more determined to figure it out.

Maybe it was an early indication of my aptitude for interrogation. If there was something I wasn't supposed to know, I couldn't rest until I knew it. I can't remember ever laughing harder than when the cop on *The Simpsons* asked his son, "What is your infatuation with the secret closet of mystery?"

Maybe it was just the natural curiosity of any adopted kid.

Either way, during the Labor Day break before my junior year of college, I went back to Enid on my own to see if I could crack the secret.

I was determined to find my birth mother and had brought enough money to stay in a hotel for three days. I figured the best place to start was the public library. I searched newspapers dated on and around my birth date, but to no avail. After a couple of hours of frustration, the kindly librarian took pity on me and steered me to the records section, where I sifted through all sorts of references—everything from phone books to yearbooks. Finally, in the court records of adoption cases, I found what I was looking for. The judge accidentally let my mother's name—Webster—slip.

We returned to the yearbooks, looking for all female Websters until finally I came across a picture of a teenage girl who had a familiar look: Debbie Webster. When the librarian saw it, her eyes welled up. "Oh my God. That has to be her."

I looked up the name in some old phonebooks and discovered that a Debbie Webster had lived in Enid at the home of Thelma Webster until 1972, the year I was born. A cross-check of a current directory showed that the address was still listed.

Now I had some soul searching to do. What was the point of this exercise? Was it to meet the mother who gave me up for adoption or was it just to prove I could find her? Either way, I had to play this out.

The Webster residence was a small, white house with a screened-in front porch. An elderly lady sat smoking a cigarette out front. She eyed me with suspicion. I was a college kid and looked the part, with brown Cole Haan loafers, white tube socks, and a Tommy Hilfiger shorts-and-shirt combination. If I saw that kid today, I'd throw an egg at him.

"Can I help you?" the lady on the porch asked me. I should have been more prepared. I hadn't actually expected to find her, and up close I couldn't see a resemblance. "Yes, hello . . . I'm, uh, looking for someone. Are you Thelma Webster?"

"Who wants to know?" she asked, still suspicious.

I took a deep breath. "I'm from Enid. I was born here and I was adopted and I think that you have a daughter, Debbie. If she had a child and gave it up for adoption, I think I'm that person."

She took another long pull off her cigarette and let the question hang in the air with the smoke for what felt like a lifetime. What was I doing here, I asked myself again. Was this a mistake? How long was that ash on her cigarette going to get before it fell off?

After a long silence she responded. "No, no, you look too old."

"May 10, 1972, does that ring a bell?" I persisted.

Finally she smiled and said, "Maybe you ought to come inside."

I blinked but stood motionless. Now I knew. I actually could have just left and been perfectly happy. They said I couldn't find her, but I did. Hell, I did it in less than eight hours.

Inside Thelma Webster told me that her daughter lived in Austin and volunteered to call her for me. I wasn't at all ready to get on the phone but couldn't find the words to stop her from making the call.

Thankfully, Debbie wasn't home. I asked Thelma if she had any pictures and she showed me several. I noted our striking resemblance in silence then asked if I could have one of the photos of my mother taken when she was in high school. She gave it to me and I thanked her. Then I left.

I never attempted to contact either my mother or grand-mother again. Finding them was enough. I keep the picture in my office and consider it to be one of my most treasured pos-sessions.

★ ★ ★

I had joined the Army to be a paratrooper. My goal was to be a "ground-pounder," a grunt. I joined the Army to serve my coun-try, and I wanted to make the most of my enlistment. Out on the front line was where wars were fought and won.

In 1995 I made it into Ranger School and it proved to be every bit as tough and demanding as I had heard. But I made it through and went on to become a squad leader for the 82nd Airborne Division. I had achieved the goals I set for myself when I first enlisted. It was time to start thinking about new objec-tives.

An interesting opportunity presented itself when I was sent to Latin America for training exercises. I started learning street Spanish from the locals. I had never considered myself especially good at learning languages, but I enjoyed the process. It prompted me to check out the Army's foreign-language pro-gram. I took the test and scored high enough to get my choice of any of the dozens of languages being taught at the Defense Language Institute in Monterey, California. I picked Mandarin Chinese. At that point I was offered two options. The first was to be a voice interceptor. That basically consisted of sitting in a windowless room with a pair of headphones listening to foreign radio transmissions. The second was to be a Mandarin Chinese interrogator. Since we weren't at war with China, the likelihood of actually interrogating anyone was pretty slim. But it was certainly preferable to sitting behind a desk monitoring broadcasts eight hours a day. So I signed on. I figured it might prove useful when I left the military and moved into the private sector. A working knowledge of Chinese could be a very marketable skill.

It was also one of the hardest languages in the world to master. Over the next eighteen months I struggled to read, write, and speak it; and, when I graduated in 1999, it was by the skin of my teeth.

There wasn't a lot of forethought that went into my decision. It wasn't as if I ever wanted to be an interrogator or even thought I had the skills to be one. But once I made the choice, I was determined to do the best I could. From that point on, I thought of myself as an interrogator and wanted to do interrogations, even though I had no idea how to go about it and wasn't likely to get the chance.

Instead I was eventually sent to Beijing, where I was attached to the U.S. Embassy as a linguist and translator. Mostly my job consisted of translating newspaper articles and escorting American VIPs around town, sometimes even bargaining for them with the local shopkeepers.

By late summer of 2000, I was back in the States, where I returned to Fort Huachuca for a course that would qualify me to become an E-6 staff sergeant. When I was there I met a woman in Tucson and we got married later that fall. We would go on to have two sons, but our marriage didn't last. In our first few years together, I deployed six times, and nearly every tour was for six months. Our very young marriage couldn't take it.

There are many effects of war, not just casualties on the battlefield. Sometimes even two good people cannot make a marriage work. Whatever the reason, it was a difficult and painful decision. Thankfully both of us were committed to the kids as our number one priority.

By the time our second son was on the way, the Army had loaned me out to a military intelligence agency. It was there that I first met Lee. We were sent on various deployments where our specific training and language skills could prove useful. I found myself increasingly desperate to take these trips.

Then came 9/11. Suddenly I knew what I was supposed to be doing: hunting down these sons-of-bitches to the farthest corners of the earth. I started making numerous requests for assignments, anywhere and everywhere. Lee, who spoke Farsi, was naturally more in demand as an interrogator and would eventually serve in Afghanistan and at Guantánamo Bay. I had to be satisfied with a string of backwater deployments, far away from the action. But when the war started and the request came down for experienced interrogators with infantry training to go to Iraq, I saw my chance. I had no hesitation in pointing out to my superiors that I had volunteered for whatever they had thrown at me. Now there was a real war going on, with a real need for interrogators for the first time in decades. I may not have had the opportunity to ever interrogate a prisoner before, but it was not for a lack of volunteering.

They saw my point. It had been a long time coming, but I was finally going to do my job.

CHAPTER 4

DOGS OF WAR

1100 30JUL2003

I woke up at 1100 feeling totally refreshed and revived. I'd only had about three hours sleep. There's something about getting shot at by a fifty-caliber machine gun that gives you a whole new appreciation of life.

Everyone else was still in the rack, so I took the opportunity to look around. Over the next few days, I'd get a complete picture of the mansion's layout. Upstairs was a large open area with rows of bunk beds. This was the shooter's quarters. Each one got both a bottom and top bunk. The bottom was to sleep on; the top was to store their weapons and equipment. There were a few couches and a TV where they played video games in their downtime. A corridor led to the operations room I'd seen on my first night, equipped with maps and computers for receiving and evaluating intelligence.

From the second floor there was a view of the mansion grounds. From the back you could see the Tigris River, down the slope of a dead lawn past the thick brush of the bank. The wide flow of the river created a natural barrier to the post.

Off to one side of the mansion was a guesthouse and behind that a large pool used by the task force. Its chlorinated blue water contrasted starkly with the dry desert in every direction.

Downstairs, past the piles of weapons and ammo in the living room, a spacious kitchen opened onto the dining room. This was the main meeting area, where everyone gathered around the big table to talk and eat. Another hallway led to two more bedrooms and a laundry area with a washer and dryer.

I was loading the few pieces of clothing I'd brought when I heard a voice behind me. "What are you doing up so early?"

I turned to face one of the guys I'd seen in the operations room last night, short and compact, with a Midwestern accent. I couldn't remember his name.

"Rich," he reminded me, sticking out his hand. "I'm the analyst around here."

It didn't take long to find out that, in the hierarchy of the house, Rich was pretty low in the pecking order. For one thing, he slept downstairs. The upstairs bunks were reserved exclusively for the shooters. Along with Chris, a case officer who ran informants, and Larry, a computer guy who passed information back to the United States, Rich was part of the intelligence team and we all slept downstairs. It was our job to gather the reliable data for the raids. As more and more dry holes started turning up—raids in which the primary target was not captured—these were the guys who would take the heat.

As we talked in the laundry room, I was able to glean more basic information. Added to what I had already gotten from Jared the terp, a clearer picture of the situation in Tikrit was emerging.

The mission of the task force, Rich told me, had been to hunt down High Value Targets. As Saddam's hometown, Tikrit had been hit hard and repeatedly. It was assumed that most of the HVTs in the area had already been rounded up or had scattered. "Right now," Rich told me, "we'll go after anyone we can find. Insurgents, Baath Party members, Saddam sympathizers." He shrugged. "As long as we're here, we've got to do something."

I thought about that for a minute, remembering Jared's theory that Saddam's bodyguards were worth taking a look at. I still had the list he'd given me in my back pocket. "So . . . are you getting close to anybody?"

"Not really. But lately we've been trying to track down a dude named Haddoushi."

"Muhammad Haddoushi?" I asked. The name rang a bell; this was the bodyguard Jared thought might still be in contact with Saddam.

I was hoping it would sound like I knew more than I did. "That's the one," he continued. "His nephew was killed when they got Uday and Qusay a few days ago. Those family links are important."

That also fit in with what the terp had told me about the relatives and tribes loyal to Saddam forming an interlocking network. "How do you get information about these people?" was my next question.

"We have sources, but they're not very reliable. Most of them were handed over to us from the guys here before us."

Voices from down the hall cut our conversation short. I followed Rich back into the dining room area, where the task force was coming in one by one for an early afternoon breakfast. I would soon learn to adjust to a schedule that started late in the day and ended early in the morning. I would also get to know who was who and what role each one played.

A half dozen highly trained soldiers were at the core of the task force. These were the men who carried out the raids. Even when they weren't on a mission they functioned as a tightly knit team. They slept in the same quarters, ate their meals together, and played video games with almost the same intensity as they did their job. They never made a big deal about their status as the military's most elite unit. That fact was already well established. And being part of that unit meant that you handled your superior status with quiet dignity and humility. But there was an unmistakable distinction between them and the rest of the world. I knew from that first morning what side of that line I was on.

Along with me on that side were Rich the analyst, Chris the case officer, and the rest of the intelligence team. This included three bodyguards who accompanied Chris when he contacted the sources providing him with their increasingly unreliable tips. Rounding out the residents were a bomb technician, a radio and communications guy, and an air tactician, whose job was to coordinate air support for the raids. Counting Jack and Matt, the first and second in command, the mansion was home to about sixteen men, give or take the occasional analyst or brass from Baghdad.

The entire team had arrived in Tikrit only three weeks before me and they were still trying to get a feel for the environment. They were on the same steep learning curve I was on just three weeks ahead of me. I listened carefully as the shooters at the dining table talked matter-of-factly about last night's raid while they ate their breakfast.

My own breakfast was an MRE—meal ready to eat. I had noticed the well-stocked refrigerator and pantry in the kitchen but I didn't know whom all that food belonged to, much less if I could help myself.

"Hey, man," said the guy with the handlebar mustache, who I would later find out was the air tactician. "We got a whole supermarket in there. You don't have to eat that shit."

The fact was, I liked MREs, providing I could pick just the best parts out of two or three of them at the same time. Right then, what had my attention was the shooters' conversation. Jeff, the Texan I'd met the night before, had come downstairs and was talking to Carl, who'd accompanied me on the raid.

"So," he asked casually, as if I wasn't even in the room. "How did Eric do last night?"

Carl nodded his approval. "Went right at the guy. Didn't even flinch when we got lit up, either."

If Jeff was the least bit impressed, he didn't show it. Instead he turned to me and said, "I don't know when you're going back, but I'd still like you to interrogate that bodyguard."

"I'm here as long as you need me. Anything I should know about the guy?"

"Fourth ID picked him up. Drunk off his ass. Supposed to be a big shot, but nobody knows for sure. Maybe you can find out."

"Okay." Despite the good report Carl had given me, I felt bad about last night. The task force had done their job. My job had been to find Nezham. I didn't know what the expectations were, but for me the bottom line was I hadn't found the guy they were looking for. Maybe I'd have better luck next time, though who knew if there was going to be a next time.

After breakfast I rode with Jeff out to the 4th ID prison where the detainee was being held. With Jared due to ship out, there was a new terp for the session, a haggard-looking Iraqi-American named Adam. He seemed harmless enough.

As the three of us drove through the sprawling 4th ID base,

Jeff gave me a brief tour. Formerly Saddam's palace complex in Tikrit, it was as big as a good-size college campus. There were up to fifty mansions, each the size of the task force quarters, and three massive castles interspersed around manmade lakes. There had once been a luxurious garden, but that had long since died from lack of attention.

"The Fourth ID controls this base camp," he told me. "We just live here. Fourth ID is responsible for most of the Sunni Triangle. They make the rules and they own the battle space. We go after the HVTs. It is as simple as that. We get whatever we want and need to find them. If a detainee or source knows something about an HVT, we get them. Other than that, Fourth ID is in charge."

Five minutes later we were at the detention facility. I didn't know what this little prison had been before; it was nothing more than a large office room with two windows and a doorway. But it worked well as a prison. There was enough space to allow thirty to fifty detainees to stay in the big room and still maintain tight security.

"Let's go see the sheriff," Jeff said as he parked the car next to the entrance, where three guards were staring into the detention room monitoring about two dozen captives.

"We'll be right back. We're going to talk to the sheriff," Jeff notified the guards and they nodded their approval. Across the way there was another building guarded by a mutt dog with a menacing snarl. The sheriff was the 4th ID staff sergeant in charge of the battalion detention facility. He informed us that the drunk bodyguard had not completely detoxed but that they did have another bodyguard who had been detained the day before. Jeff and I agreed that talking to anyone was better than no one at all. So the sheriff released the bodyguard to us and we watched as the prisoner was handcuffed with thin plastic zip ties and an empty sandbag was placed over his head. We put him in the backseat with Adam and returned to the task force headquarters.

Jeff, who had done most of the interrogations before I came, had used the mansion's guesthouse for questioning detainees. It was there that we took the bodyguard. The place was well suited for the task at hand. It had four bedrooms, the largest of which had a couple of couches, some plastic folding chairs, and a piece of plywood propped on ration boxes to serve as a table. The windows were also covered with plywood but what really made it ideal was the air-conditioning. Considering the long hours spent in there, and the intensity of the work being done, air-conditioning was essential to cope with the 120-degree heat.

"So how do you want to handle this?" Jeff was being polite by asking me first, but I knew the meaning behind his words: You're the interrogator. This is where you earn your keep.

"I'm flexible. I figured I'd just start. Any time you want to jump in is fine with me. Maybe we can take a break every hour or so, to give the terp a rest and evaluate where we're at."

Jeff agreed. I knew I needed him in there with me. First, he knew more about the situation on the ground than I did. But equally important was the fact that I wanted to be able to gain his trust in my ability to interrogate. Not that I exactly trusted myself. I didn't know what the hell I was doing.

But this really wasn't about proving anything to him, or to anyone else. I had to be totally focused on getting information, information the task force could use. As of that moment I had no idea what this handcuffed man with a bag on his head might be able to tell me, or if he'd tell me anything at all. I was looking for something. I just had no idea what it was.

I could feel Jeff and Adam's eyes on me as I sat down and removed the bag from the prisoner's head. I took a deep breath. Those few minutes I'd spent last night in the chaos and confusion of the raid were just a warm-up. Now I needed to earn my keep.

★ ★ ★

The prisoner's name was Rafi Idham Ibrahim Al-Hasan Al-Tikriti. Rafi was the name his parent's gave him; Idham was his father; Ibrahim was his grandfather; Al-Hasan was his tribe and Al-Tikriti identified his hometown. His name alone provided some useful information.

The rest would be up to me. And I wanted to find out as much as I could. I was new to the job, new to the country, new to the war. To me Rafi was more than a detainee; he was a walking encyclopedia. He could tell me what it was like to be an Iraqi, a Muslim, a Sunni. He could describe the world of a bodyguard and take me inside their inner circle. I needed to hear it all. But most of all, I needed to learn what it meant to be an interrogator. This was my chance for some on-the-job training.

From the beginning I had my doubts about my prisoner. He was a former lieutenant colonel in the Iraqi army, but he looked like he was more familiar with taking orders than giving them. Hunched and frail, he acted polite and eager to please, ready to tell me anything he thought I wanted to hear. As time went on and I gained more experience interrogating, I would learn the detainees with balls were actually the best subjects. They didn't just tell you what they thought you wanted to hear. Instead they'd test and challenge you in a game of wits to see who would prevail. When you went toe to toe with them, at least you had the chance to catch them in a lie. The weak and passive ones were only interested in placating you and staying out of trouble. You had to move past their fear and submission to even have a chance of getting at the truth. For the moment, all Rafi wanted us to know was how happy he was to be fully cooperating with the liberators of his country.

"How do you feed your family, Rafi?" I asked him once I'd gotten the preliminaries out of the way—mostly routine questions about his background. He answered with a longwinded story about how he had retired from the military, had gone into farming and was then drafted back into service in the run-up to the war. It was all pretty vague, but I preferred it that way, even though it took hours to get through. I wanted to know what he was most afraid to tell us.

"What did you do when you left the military?" I asked.

He went on to disavow any knowledge or connection to the regime. "I only worked at the palace," he insisted.

"Not where, Rafi. What? What did you do?"

"Hamaya," he muttered. It was the Arabic word for "bodyguard." After several hours going around in circles we were finally getting somewhere.

"Whose bodyguard?" I asked, already knowing the answer. Rafi glanced around the room, like he was looking for a way out.

"Whose bodyguard!" I repeated loudly.

Rafi flinched. "I was the lowest bodyguard for the president," he whispered.

"Say 'Saddam,' asshole!" Adam shouted. "He's not the president anymore." Adam was proving his worth as a terp. He sensed the purpose behind my tactics and actually seemed to be getting angry along with me.

I let a moment pass in silence. I wanted Rafi to think about where this was going. "We know you were Saddam's bodyguard," I said at last. "I just wanted to see how long you were going to avoid telling me."

"I was not avoiding you, mister," he insisted. "I was ashamed that they made me come back."

"What was your job in the army, before the war?"

"I am a retired lieutenant colonel."

"I didn't ask for your rank," I barked, inches from his face. "I asked what your fucking job was!"

"Hamaya." His voice was barely audible.

"So you were ashamed to come back to take a job you'd already done for twenty years?" I asked with maximum sarcasm.

"I was the lowest bodyguard," he repeated helplessly.

"How is it that you were a lieutenant colonel and still just an insignificant bodyguard?"

"I was related to Saddam. He gave me the rank."

As soon as the words came out of his mouth, Rafi realized he'd made a serious mistake. This was the one fact he definitely didn't want us to know.

"How are you related to Saddam?" I asked, dropping my voice and looking him in the eye.

"My grandfather took care of him," he answered very slowly and carefully. "My father was close to him."

"I want to know how *you* are related."

"Mister, there is no blood between us."

For the first time Jeff spoke up, telling Rafi clearly how he was sick of his pathetic groveling attitude, his lies and even his annoying personality. Jeff's deep-set eyes were flashing and his jaw was clenched. It was the first time I'd seen his temper flare, but it wouldn't be the last.

Over the next hour we both worked on the prisoner until we had gotten all the details of his family tree. By that time, it was clear that Rafi was closer to Saddam than we could have expected. He was, in fact, a nephew once removed. His father, Rafi told me, was Saddam's oldest and dearest stepbrother, and Rafi's dad was like a father to Saddam.

"But I hate Saddam," Rafi insisted. "I will kill him myself. Thank you, mister, for saving my country. Together we will make a powerful team to bring down the regime."

"Bring down the regime?" I repeated, "You *are* the regime, Rafi. You're Saddam's nephew and one of his bodyguards. Do you know what that means?"

"But I hate—"

"Shut the fuck up!" Jeff shouted.

In any interrogation, one of the primary purposes is to establish guilt. In a war like the one we were fighting, when the enemy was everywhere and nowhere, that could prove extremely difficult. It was more than convincing yourself that the person you were questioning was a bad guy. You had to convince him of the fact. By revealing his close connection to Saddam, Rafi had also revealed that he had been trying to deceive us every chance he had. "We got you, Rafi," I continued. "We've got enough to put you in prison for the rest of your life."

"But I want to help," he whined.

"So help. Help me help you." I leaned in again. "I don't like you, Rafi. You've done nothing but waste my time. This is your last chance. Give me a reason to help you. If I don't help you, nobody else will."

I was working purely on instinct. It was only later, after a lot of trial and error, that I realized I had come to a critical juncture in the interrogation process. This was the plea bargaining phase.

We knew, and Rafi knew, that he was in trouble. My job was to convince him that honesty and cooperation was the better alternative to definite, long-term confinement. Once I'd made my pitch, I just kept repeating it to make sure he understood, and that nothing was going to happen one way or the other until he made his decision.

★ ★ ★

I had learned some valuable lessons in the hours I'd spent questioning Rafi. The most important was the value of complete sincerity. Whatever you were feeling at any given moment—anger, sympathy, even boredom—it had to be real. Otherwise they'd see right through you. Every emotion was operating at its peak level and it was essential to maintain that intensity. For a detainee, an interrogation is the most important moment of his life. His fate is hanging in the balance. An interrogator has to understand that and treat the situation accordingly.

At the same time I had to formulate each question and anticipate where the answers would lead. I was trying to stay a few steps ahead of the process, without seeming too calculated. I was also beginning to see the benefit of simply talking in a way that didn't grate or irritate. Whether I was being reasonable or pissed off, what mattered was that my tone of voice didn't get in the way of connecting with the prisoner.

These techniques came in handy as I continued the interrogation. After a few hours, Rafi began to give up more information. I knew what the ultimate goal was: to get actionable intelligence for the task force to do their job. That was one reason Jeff's participation was so important. If our interrogation actually produced a lead, he'd have as much time and effort invested in the results as I did.

But in the meantime, I was also getting a better understanding of Saddam's network of bodyguards. As my questioning continued, I pressed Rafi for details on the system. There were, he explained, three levels of bodyguards. The innermost circle was with the leader at all times. The second circle would usually secure locations in advance of Saddam's travels throughout the country. The third circle was assigned to fixed locations. Rafi, for example, claimed to be the night shift guard at one of Saddam's Baghdad palaces. But as helpful as Rafi's information might have been, it wasn't getting the task force any closer to real targets. It was time for me to step aside and let Jeff do his thing.

"Where are the terrorists?' he asked Rafi, as if we were starting the whole process all over again.

"Terrorists?" Rafi asked with wide-eyed innocence.

Now it was Jeff's turn to get in his face. "Listen, fucker," he hissed. "American soldiers are getting shot at every day around here. Who's doing it? Tell me or I swear to God I'll die before you see the light of day again."

"But I don't know any terror—"

"Stop!" I jumped up, shouting. I didn't want to hear those words coming out of his mouth. Once he was committed to that version of his story—that he had no knowledge or connection to the insurgency—I was sure he'd stick with it. He didn't want to be caught lying again, and the last thing I wanted was to back him into that particular corner. I started talking fast, to keep him from trying to tell us what he didn't know. "I have a job to do, Rafi. It's very simple. I need to catch the bad guys. If I do my job, my boss will like me. If you help me do my job, I will like you. Then I will help you. Do you want me to help you, Rafi?"

He nodded meekly.

"I know you do. And the way you can help me is to give me the names and locations of as many terrorists as you can."

"I want to say something," he interjected before I stopped him again.

"Rafi, I'm going to let you speak. But please don't tell me that you don't know any terrorists." I took a deep breath. "Now, what are you never, ever going to tell me again?"

"I am never going to tell you that I don't know any terrorists."

"Good," I said. "So what do you want to say?"

"I want to say that when I am free, I hope you will not forget my name and that we can work together for many years to come."

"Why would I set you free, Rafi?"

"Because I am innocent."

I let myself get angry again. "Do I care about your innocence?" I shouted. "I only care about one thing, Rafi. What is that?" He looked confused and frightened. "My job, you shithead! That's all I care about!" I stood over the prisoner and barked. "What is my job, Rafi?"

"To catch the bad guys, mister," he replied, trembling.

"Are you going to help me catch the bad guys, Rafi?"

There was a long pause. I could almost see the wheels turning in his head. When he finally spoke, it was barely above a whisper. "Mister, I have heard things but I don't know for certain. I don't want to bring trouble if I haven't seen it with my own eyes."

"You're already in trouble, Rafi. Tell me what you heard."

He looked from Jeff to me and back again. I could see him squirming, his mouth gaping like a fish out of water, trying to form the words. "Two men," he said at last. "They work at a car wash. They hate Americans."

★ ★ ★

Once he got over that hurdle, it turned out that Rafi had more information. He claimed that there were, at most, only three men remaining in Tikrit who had been connected with the regime. Rafi also knew their jobs, their family members, and where they had lived. As interesting as this was, I was getting increasingly frustrated and so was Jeff. During a break he told me that the men Rafi had named were insignificant during the regime and were likely to be even more insignificant now. According to Rafi, every other important person he knew had either fled or already been captured. He kept insisting he had no idea where we could find any active insurgents. I was beginning to wonder just how helpful this prisoner could be. Wouldn't it already be well known that he was in American custody? Wouldn't the insurgents have already changed their locations and routines as a precaution? Even if Rafi knew where they were, wouldn't they be long gone? But I kept my doubts to myself. I wanted Rafi to think that he was giving us what we wanted, to keep alive his hope of being freed.

It was midnight before we finished with Rafi and took him back to the prison. Back at the house, Jeff and I compared notes on the interrogation.

"What do you think?" Jeff asked me. Behind the simple question was another test. I was the professional interrogator. He wanted to hear my "expert" analysis.

"I don't think there's any way that guy doesn't know something," I said. "He's a former bodyguard and a nephew of Saddam. But three former low-level guys in the regime who are now working at a car wash aren't what we're looking for."

"Yeah," Jeff agreed. He sounded as tired as I was. "That shit was weak. But I'll run it by Matt and Jack and see what they think."

I headed to the dining room for something to eat. I needed to think over what had just happened. On one level the interrogation had been a failure. We hadn't gotten actionable intelligence, at least as far as I could tell. Maybe Rafi really didn't know anything. Or maybe he did and I just hadn't pried it out of him.

But, in another way, I was exhilarated by the experience. For the first time since I'd signed up for the job, I realized that I had an innate capability to be an interrogator. I may not have known exactly how to do it yet, but I knew I could do it.

As I sat alone at the table, I reviewed all the mistakes I had made over the last several hours. I had asked unnecessary questions; let Rafi see where I was going before I got there; lost my temper when I should have stayed calm and vice versa. I now had firsthand experience in some of the many ways to screw up an interrogation. I couldn't tell myself that I wouldn't make the same mistake twice, but at least I knew what the mistakes were. Slowly I was beginning to learn how to keep the details straight; how to close out the paths of evasion and how not to let a prisoner see the traps I was laying for him. I was beginning to understand not just how to ask questions but *why* I was asking the questions. Raw information was less important than what that information told me about the prisoner I was questioning: what he was thinking, what he was afraid of, what he had to hide. The point wasn't just to catch him in a lie. I would quickly come to realize that most of what my prisoners told me were lies. It was the *reason* they were lying that was important.

At the same time, I had begun to painstakingly put together a picture of Tikrit. Rafi had his version of the city. The next guy

I interrogated would have another version, with maybe a little overlap. If they let me stay, maybe I'd eventually find the way it all fit together.

I had no reason to think they'd keep me. My original assignment had been for forty-eight hours and that was almost up. The only reason for me to stay on was if I proved myself useful and, so far, that hadn't happened.

I started going over the fifteen pages of notes I'd taken during Rafi's interrogation. I was hoping there was something I might have missed, something I could point to in the report I would write the next morning. I'd wanted to make it lengthy and detailed to demonstrate my added value to the mission. But after scanning my almost unreadable scrawl, it was depressingly clear that it could all be summed in a few sentences: Rafi Idham Ibrahim Al-Hasan Al-Tikriti is a nephew and former bodyguard of Saddam. He provided no actionable information. It was determined that he was not honest during questioning. He should not be released until hell or Tikrit freezes over. By the way, this team might need a better interrogator.

CHAPTER 5

THE ROUTINE

1400 31JUL2003

I wasn't sure whether anyone noticed that I had overstayed my assignment in Tikrit, or if anyone even cared. In the days following my interrogation of Rafi, I was still hoping to convince the team to keep me around.

When I approached Rich for advice on how to extend my stay, he smiled. "So you like it out here in the shit," he said.

He was right. I did. But it was more than that. "I like doing my job," I replied. "And you've got prisoners here, lots of them."

"Mostly we just ship them back to Baghdad."

"I know. But they aren't getting interrogated down there." As I had seen during my short stay in Baghdad, detainees arriving from outside of Baghdad were being sent to the back of the line. "You're not their top priority," I continued. "They don't know what to ask Tikrit prisoners, anyway. Let me stick around, Rich, and I'll interrogate everybody you bring in. You all won't have to depend on Baghdad. And they'll be happy because they will have that much less to deal with."

"How long do you want to stay?"

I shrugged. "I just started a six-month deployment."

He gave a low whistle. "We're only here for three. Tell you what. I'll talk to Matt and Jack. They'll make the call."

I figured that talking to Rich was as good a place as any to make my case for staying in Tikrit. But Jeff saw it differently. "You run that shit by me first!" he told me angrily when I informed him that I'd approached Rich. I was quickly finding that you had to tread lightly around Jeff. He had a hair-trigger temper and it didn't help that, like the rest of the shooters, he had no use for the intelligence personnel. I'd just gotten another lesson in the task force hierarchy. I knew my time was limited. Now I feared I had widened the hole in the hourglass.

I waited nervously to see how badly I had screwed up. But it seemed that I'd been granted a reprieve. Days went by with no one asking why I wasn't back in Baghdad. Meanwhile, I kept interrogating the detainees that the team brought in from their frequent raids. The yield of good intelligence was low, but at least I was getting an opportunity to prove my worth.

Jeff and I did many of the interrogations together, and I gained a lot of admiration for him. He seemed to recognize what I was trying to get done, sometimes even before I did, and gave me the freedom to do it. Sometimes the shooters would drop by the guesthouse to watch me at work. Most of them got bored and drifted off after an hour or two. But Jeff would hang in, watching patiently while I developed my strategy and asking questions of his own that were right on target. We were a good team.

I was kept very busy and in the process, I established a procedure to deal with the long interrogation sessions. My off hours were spent going over my notes, absorbing what I'd learned, if anything, from each detainee. Since I didn't really have any place

I was supposed to be, I mostly hung out at the dining room table. There were occasional visitors, primarily intelligence analysts in for debriefings on the local situation. Otherwise the house was divided into rigid categories: those of us who slept downstairs and those who slept upstairs.

The shooters had a regular rhythm to their days, too, consisting of exercise, video games, weapons maintenance, and time spent at the firing range. Then came the intense energy and adrenalin of the nighttime raids.

I had my own job to do, although how I was going to get it done was an open question. When I first arrived, I spent a lot of time going over the list of bodyguards that Jared the terp had given me. Since there was no background information or rankings of importance, it was of limited use. But I did take notice of how the names were grouped into separate clans.

For instance, Nezham, the guy we had gone after my first night, was one of over thirty Al-Muslit family members on the list, all of them bodyguards. And I had learned from Rafi that anyone in the Al-Hasan tribe was related to Saddam. But names and family links were only going to get me so far. I had to connect them to faces, personalities, and possible links to the insurgency.

The next day I had a chance to interrogate the hard-drinking bodyguard I'd come to question in the first place. He was also an Al-Muslit named Adnan and he lived up to his billing. Extremely hungover, Adnan looked miserable when we arrived to pick him up from the 4th ID prison. The medics there told us to keep giving him water to make sure he didn't dehydrate from all the alcohol he hadn't finished sleeping off.

From the beginning Adnan proved more cooperative than Rafi, with none of the fake bowing and scraping. Even though he insisted on his total innocence, he seemed to understand that he wouldn't be getting out of prison and back to the bottle until he told us what he knew. He admitted to being a major in the Hamaya. He also readily acknowledged that he knew Rafi, but claimed that, despite what Rafi had told us, he was not a low-level functionary, but rather an inner-circle bodyguard. It was one more indication of the deception and evasion that was standard procedure for prisoners. There were always at least three versions to any one story, if not more.

But Adnan had other information, as well. From his straightforward willingness to answer questions, I got the feeling he was telling the truth. His alcohol-addled brain didn't seem capable of deception.

When I asked him if he knew Nezham, the target of the raid I'd gone on my first night, he freely admitted to being a distant cousin.

"Was he inner circle, too?" I asked.

He shook his head. "But his cousins were."

"Which of Nezham's cousins were Hamaya?" I continued, trying to remember the Al-Muslit names on the list.

Adnan considered for a moment. "Radman," he said. "And Khalil . . . and Muhammad Ibrahim."

"Where are they now?"

He shrugged. "Some of them lived in New Oja. But they are gone now."

New Oja was an enclave especially built by Saddam for his most important relatives in Tikrit. It gave a new meaning to the term "gated community." They had been concentrated there to be more easily watched over and couldn't move away without the dictator's permission. The neighborhood had been hit numerous times by U.S. forces since the invasion. It was unlikely that a High Value Target would still be there.

I was more interested in that cluster of Al-Muslit brothers who had served as bodyguards. I made a mental note of them with no idea whether I'd ever hear their names again. But I soon had another priority. A former housekeeper for Saddam had been rolled up and delivered to the guesthouse for questioning.

The guy turned out to be one of the most interesting subjects I would interrogate during my tour of duty in Iraq. It wasn't because he had any vital information about the insurgency or the locations of HVTs. Instead, he spent hours providing us with the most minute details on the daily life of the dictator.

His name was Tashin and, as Saddam's personal servant, his primary responsibility was serving meals. Saddam would normally eat twice a day, at two in the afternoon and seven or eight in the evening. His favorite food by far was a fish called mazgoof. Caught in the Tigris River, it was packed with salt and roasted over an open fire. Saddam couldn't get enough of it. It was all more raw data for the memory banks: Saddam liked mazgoof. Maybe these bits and pieces would come in handy one day.

Eventually I was able to turn the talk about Saddam's dining habits toward those who were in proximity to him on a daily basis. During Tashin's interrogations, one name in particular stood out: Muhammad Haddoushi. Aside from being able to make world class mazgoof, Haddoushi was known as one of Saddam's closest friends. In fact, he was even called "Little Saddam." That caught my attention. For a man who seemed to trust no one outside his immediate family circle, a real friend was a rare thing. I wanted to know more about this guy.

It didn't take long. Shortly after my session with Saddam's servant Tashin, I sat in on an interrogation conducted by two visiting intelligence analysts, Ray and Christy. It was an opportunity for me to watch someone else in action. I was hoping to pick up some tips from professionals who, I assumed, knew more than I did. It turned out to be instructive, although not exactly the way I'd thought it would.

The detainee was a short, round-faced former bodyguard named Taha. He was obviously nervous, sweating profusely. The two analysts did nothing to set him at ease or encourage him to open up.

"We know a lot about you, Taha," Ray began in an even, measured voice. "And you are in big trouble."

That would not have been my approach. The point was to find out what the prisoner knew, not tell them how much you knew. From my viewpoint, Christy wasn't helping the process by interjecting stray facts about Taha's family connections. Her knowledge of his family tree was impressive, but I couldn't see the point in revealing it. It was one thing for a prisoner to think that you knew every detail of his life. It was another thing to actually tell a prisoner what you knew. That would enable him to anticipate which areas he could or could not lie to you about.

It wasn't long before the analyst's all-knowing approach backfired. After an evasive answer from the former bodyguard, Ray accused him of being a liar. "I have told you everything," Taha declared and turned to Christy. "Ask her. She knows all the answers already." After that the session went downhill fast. I came to the conclusion that, when it came to interrogation techniques, I'd stick to my own approach.

★ ★ ★

After the analysts had finished, I stayed behind to ask Taha a few questions. I started with a rundown of his family and he revealed that two of his brothers, Farris and Nasir, had worked as

Saddam's bodyguards. I made a note of the names, adding them to my mental tally of Hamaya.

I focused next on Muhammad Haddoushi, the expert maz-goof cook and Saddam's closest friend. I wanted to see if this bodyguard would confirm what Tashin, Saddam's servant, had been telling me.

Taha not only knew exactly who Haddoushi was, he added other interesting details. Although he was not a military or government man, Haddoushi had been a major player in Tikrit before the war. He had overseen all of Saddam's homes and palaces and had maintained a large entourage of his own trusted friends and advisers.

I wanted more names. Turning up the pressure, I asked him whom else he knew who had been connected to Haddoushi. "He had a driver whose brother was arrested," Taha recalled. "The driver's brother was a servant of Saddam, whose name was Tashin."

I sat straight up. Jeff and I had previously spent hours with Saddam's personal servant Tashin, some of it talking specifically about Haddoushi. Somehow he had neglected to provide this tidbit of information. Tashin, the servant of Saddam, had a brother who was Haddoushi's driver. As I said earlier, it didn't surprise or concern me when prisoners lied to me. Figuring out the information they were trying to conceal behind the lie was what mattered.

I told Jeff what I'd learned and we had Tashin brought back to the guesthouse. "Your fucking brother was Muhammad Haddoushi's driver," Jeff informed him. "We talked about Little Saddam for hours and you didn't mention it?"

I sat staring at him as he progressively grew more nervous. Tashin swallowed hard. He was having trouble talking.

"Where is your brother now?" I asked.

"At home."

"You're going to take us to him."

"Of course. He will be happy to help," Tashin replied weakly.

"Oh, I'm sure he's going to be thrilled to see us," I said dryly.

The next night we raided the house of Tashin's brother and picked him up. He was tall for an Iraqi, over six feet and well groomed with a neat beard and white clothing that contrasted with his dark skin. Back at the guesthouse, he seemed only too willing to tell us anything we wanted to know about the man he once worked for.

He confirmed that Muhammad Haddoushi's nephew had been shot in the raid that had taken out Saddam's sons, Uday and Qusay. Haddoushi himself had almost been killed in a raid a few days later but had managed to escape.

"Where is he now?" I asked.

"Maybe at one of his houses," the driver suggested.

"How many houses does he have?"

"Eight all together. And he is building another."

I thought for a moment. It didn't seem likely that Haddoushi would be hiding in one of his own places. "Anywhere else he might be?" I asked. "A friend's house, maybe?"

The driver nodded. There was one man Haddoushi was closer to than all the rest—Salam Shaban. It was one of the same names Taha had given me hours earlier.

I returned to the main house and, tracking down Rich, passed on what I had learned over the course of several interrogations. By the next morning Rich, using a military version of Google Earth called Falcon View, had located the house of

Shaban on overhead imagery, based on a sketch from Tashin's brother. The team was in the final planning stages of a hit for that evening; they would soon be launching a round up of all the Haddoushi homes the driver had identified for us as well.

I had no idea where all this was heading. But it was starting to get fun.

CHAPTER 6

ROUNDUP

1200 04AUG2003

The fact that I had been involved in interrogations that were about to lead to significant raids was good news. I had moved a few steps closer to proving my worth to the task force. At least I hoped so. But I still worried about being sent back to Baghdad.

I was sitting at the dining room table as usual, going over my notes, when Jeff and the team's two senior men, Matt and Jack, sat down on either side of me. "So, Eric," Jack asked casually, "what did they tell you back in Baghdad about how long you'd be staying up here?"

After five days of trying to prove my usefulness by keeping as busy as possible, this was the chance I'd been waiting for. Whatever the right answer was, I needed to be ready to provide it. But at the same time, I didn't want to appear overeager. The last thing these guys wanted was eager. The one quality everyone on the task force shared was a cool, calm approach to the job at hand. On a raid, for example, too much enthusiasm could get someone killed. As an interrogator my job was to provide intelligence. The rest of the time I needed to stay out of the way.

"They didn't say anything," I responded. "But I think I can be of more use here than I was back at BIAP."

"Why's that?" Matt asked.

"I need to get my arms around something," I told him. "That's how I work most effectively. In Baghdad it's hard to know what's going on. It's too big to really get a handle on. Every new prisoner has another story. Here in Tikrit, the pieces should be starting to connect. The city is only so big."

They looked at each other, silently sizing up their options. "Look," Jack said at last. "We're going to do the Haddoushi raid in a few days. I can keep you around until then."

In the wake of the initial series of interrogations, the size and scope of the Haddoushi raid had expanded considerably. The list of eight houses we had identified had grown to almost twenty, including the locations of various "persons of interest."

That list had grown, too. The night after our interrogation of Haddoushi's driver, the task force had picked up Salam Shaban, who had been identified as one of Haddoushi's closest friends. The raid itself couldn't have been simpler: we drove up to his house and Adam the terp got on a bullhorn and ordered him to come out with his hands up. An elderly and well-dressed gentleman emerged a moment later and immediately volunteered to return to the compound with us. Over the next few hours Shaban told me a lot about Haddoushi. He gave us the names of a whole group of Little Saddam's buddies who would be invited to feasts hosted by Haddoushi when Saddam was in Tikrit before the war. Haddoushi was described as friendly, outgoing, and a real party animal, providing hookers along with his famous mazgoof.

With the new names and locations, the scope of the roundup grew. The task force requested extra assistance from conventional forces of the 4th ID. The additional manpower required more planning. The details would take time to finalize.

Eventually a routine was established. I'd get up around ten A.M. and spend a few hours going over my notes or hanging out with the operators. They were always busy, repairing vehicles, working out in the gym, or making various improvements on the house. At about noon I started with my first interrogation of the day and work until about 4:30. After dinner, at around 7:30, I'd go back to the guesthouse and continue interrogating until 12:30 that night. Then I'd spend another hour analyzing what we had learned with Jeff before I went to sleep and started all over again the next morning.

One afternoon, shortly before the scheduled roundup, I was sitting in the dining room after a long day of interrogating some low-level detainees. By this time I felt comfortable enough to sample some of the food from the refrigerator. The fact that nobody called me on it seemed like an encouraging sign that, slowly but surely, I was finding my place in the house.

Then, suddenly, my position didn't seem so secure. I looked up to see the grinning face of another interrogator, with a duffel bag slung over his shoulder. His name was Allen and I had worked with him briefly at BIAP. What was he doing here?

"Hey, what's going on?" I asked, trying to sound nonchalant.

"Just got in," he replied, dropping his bag and coming over to pick the leftovers off my plate. He was still grinning, an expression I remembered from our time together in Baghdad. I hadn't gotten a good impression of Allen the arrogant. He had an attitude and wasn't a team player.

"What brings you out here?"

"They need support for some big raid," he replied, still chewing.

"I thought you guys were real busy down at BIAP." I didn't like where this was going.

He shrugged. "I speak the language," he said. "I guess I'm in demand," he added condescendingly.

I'd forgotten about that. Allen was fluent in Arabic. Suddenly I had competition. And he had a definite advantage. I tried to tell myself that there was nothing to worry about. He was just here for the roundup. But I still felt uneasy. The realization of just how much I wanted to stay in Tikrit, to continue the work I started, took on new significance. After only two weeks, I felt like Tikrit was the right place to be. More important, the team needed me as much as I needed them. I liked my job. And I was getting better at it every day. Allen's arrival might put an end to that before it really even began. Where before I was paranoid my time was limited, now I could see my stay in Tikrit had an expiration date.

✷ ✷ ✷

It was mid-August and well over a hundred degrees in the shade. The blistering heat had figured into the planning for the Haddoushi roundup. The raids had been set for the eleventh of the month at 1400, the hottest part of the day. The reason was simple: everyone would be in their homes, taking naps to escape the scorching midday sun. The streets would be empty, making it easier for us to move through the city. The targets would more likely be at the locations we'd identified. Jeff had a name for it: the witch hunting hours.

That morning, the pace of preparations increased. Another element of the task force had arrived from Baghdad to assist in the operation. The house was crowded and I could tell by the muffled music in the shooters' headphones that they were getting themselves ready. There was always more metal rock in the hours before a hit.

I was walking back from the guesthouse, where a small gym had been set up. Exercise was my way of preparing myself and, unlike the shooters, I was nervous and excited about going on the hit. I had at least something to do with bringing this engagement about. More than anything I hoped we would be rolling up Muhammad Haddoushi before the day was over.

I heard a honk and turned to see Matt and Jack pulling up behind me.

"We've been talking to that guy you worked with back at BIAP," Jack told me from the open window of the SUV.

"Yeah. Allen," I said, with a sinking feeling in the pit of my stomach.

He nodded. "He said he'd be willing to relocate up here to Tikrit."

That was the last thing I wanted to hear. But it got worse.

"We don't need two interrogators, Eric," Matt added, leaning over from the passenger seat. "They won't allow it."

"So you want *me* to leave?" I sounded pathetic even to myself.

"The guy speaks Arabic," Jack said. "We wouldn't need a terp with him. He could do the interrogations here and we could use Adam for the raids."

I couldn't think of anything to say. There was no reason for them to keep me, except for my vague intuition about bodyguards. And that wasn't good enough. It was easy to see that they didn't care one way or the other. I was interchangeable with Allen as far as they were concerned. They just wanted the job done, as simply and straightforwardly as possible. Suddenly everything slowed to a crawl. My thoughts arrived in slow motion. I envisioned the last grain of sand in the hourglass freefalling with a thud, marking the end of my time in Tikrit.

I stepped back as they drove away. I'd had a good run. I'd learned more about interrogating in the time I'd spent here than anything they'd taught me at school. But it still felt like a kick in the front of the shorts. I was just getting up to speed, feeling my way through the labyrinth of the city, following leads wherever they took me. Now I'd be going back behind the wire of the BIAP where it didn't really matter what I did or how well I did it.

★ ★ ★

It had to have been close to 120 degrees when we finally left the compound for the Haddoushi roundup. It felt even hotter in the back of the armored Humvee where I was sitting. The scorching wind blowing in my face felt like a blast furnace and I was relieved when we reached the objective within five minutes. Grateful as I was to have the wind out of my face, I didn't have time to think about what we might be driving into. Sometimes ignorance is bliss.

The team I was with, which included a terp we had borrowed from the 4th ID, took up positions at opposite ends of a street where one of Little Saddam's houses was located. Our job was to move along both sides and link up in the middle, emptying out all the houses along the way. Two blocks over, another team, using Adam as their terp, was deployed the same way.

The 4th ID terp was given a bullhorn to order everyone onto the street and my job was to interrogate as many as possible, to either identify the bad guys or find out where they were.

As the shooters jumped out of the Humvees and took their positions, the terp starting barking commands into the bullhorn. The only problem was, the bullhorn did not work. Unsure what to do, he just kept talking into the dead mouthpiece while everyone waited for something to happen. Standing next to him, I tried to get things moving.

"Just yell," I told him. "Get up and yell as loud as you can." He looked confused but did what I told him. Nobody was coming out onto the street. "Louder!" I urged him.

It was then that I caught of glimpse of Matt staring at me from the front of the Humvee. If a look could have blistered paint, that would have been it. I immediately understood that I had made a serious mistake. I was attached to the finest military unit in the world and I had taken it upon myself to intervene in a contingency situation. We were in the middle of a large-scale hit with a lot of moving pieces and the distinct possibility of shots being fired. It was not my place to make a decision on the raid. I was way out of line.

Fortunately by this point people were starting to emerge onto the street, so I began interrogating them. The task force rounded up the adult males and brought them to me. We'd moved as a group to the next house and after about a half hour, we met up with the second half of our team in the middle of the block.

We had about a dozen detainees by then, handcuffed and blindfolded, gathered in a backyard. Adding the men captured by the other team, we formed a lineup. We quickly questioned them until we found one who admitted to knowing Haddoushi and his family and had him identify as many of the prisoners as possible. We had netted a couple of Little Saddam's brothers-in-law, some cousins and a nephew. But no Muhammad

Haddoushi. I wasn't sure what the other teams would turn up at the remaining houses, but as far as I was concerned, we'd hit another dry hole.

By 1730 that afternoon the raids were over. We were back at the compound conducting an after action review (AAR). A lieutenant colonel had come from Baghdad for the raids. Even though we all had our doubts, the officer proclaimed the operation a success. The reason was simple, if not exactly on point. Haddoushi may have eluded us, but the roundup had netted four other wanted men. They weren't the HVTs from the deck of cards, but instead were on another list of three hundred former regime members and Saddam sympathizers.

I understood the value of these targets, but still wondered how the roundup could be considered a success when the guy we were after hadn't been nabbed. The more I thought about it, the more it seemed that there was a flaw in our approach. Taking one-time government and military personnel off the streets wasn't getting us any closer to the HVTs who were our real objectives. Those three hundred names were part of the old order in Iraq, the one we had already overthrown. There was a new network now, the one tasked with hiding Saddam and killing Americans. Maybe these guys were part of that network. Maybe not. But instead of just arresting them and congratulating ourselves on a job well done, we needed to go deeper. We needed to focus on anyone and everyone who could tell us the names of the real bad guys. That's why we'd gone after Haddoushi in the first place, not for what he'd done. He hadn't even been a full-fledged member of the regime. It was the intel he could provide that made him a prime target. Because Haddoushi's nephew had been killed with Saddam's sons Uday and Qusay, we thought he might be privy to Saddam's current whereabouts.

Not that my assumptions made any difference. I was just the interrogator. The brass were satisfied with the results, with a few exceptions.

"Listen," the lieutenant colonel concluded, "I'm not sure what to say about the AD that happened out there today. I guess we just have to remember the simple rules: selector switch on safety and finger out of the trigger well."

I bolted upright. An accidental discharge? Someone had unintentionally fired his weapon? That was unheard of among the task force and easily one of the most serious infractions one could commit. As the meeting broke up I hurried over to Jeff. "What happened with the AD?" I asked.

He pulled me aside. "It was Allen," he told me. "That interrogator from Baghdad."

I could hardly believe my ears. Allen the arrogant was now AD Allen.

"How did it happen?"

"He was talking to some ladies and shot right at their feet."

"And that means?"

"Eric," he replied. "If an operator has an AD, he's out. Period. Sorry, but your pal is history."

As it turned out, the day wasn't a total loss. Allen's quick trigger had inadvertently plugged the hourglass.

CHAPTER 7

FEAR UP HARSH

1800 12AUG2003

I had been in Tikrit for just over two weeks, working a constant schedule of interrogations. There were valuable lessons to be learned every time, as much from my failures as my successes. Except that in my situation, success was hard to define. Since I didn't really know what I was looking for, I wouldn't have recognized it if I had found it. So I just kept plugging away, piling up information and trying to make sense of it.

For every prisoner who gave me a piece of valuable information, there were ten who gave me nothing at all. Maybe they didn't have anything to begin with. Or maybe I just didn't know how to get it out of them. It was trial and error, hit and miss. But I was definitely developing my own approach.

I compared what I was getting from detainees to what was being supplied by the informants to the case officers. I was more inclined to believe what the prisoners were telling me. For one thing, I knew what their motivation was. I was providing it. I had control over their lives: their freedom and their future. That gave them a real incentive to tell me the truth.

But there was also a definite disadvantage to the intelligence we gleaned from interrogations. From the moment they were captured, there was a time limit on any information a prisoner had. Once news traveled that he was in custody, the clock was ticking. After forty-eight hours at the latest, whatever bad guys he knew about would have gone into hiding or changed up their daily routine. For that reason I had to get what I was after as soon as I could and pass it along to Jack and Matt.

As I started refining my own method of questioning, I began to realize that it was different from the standard operating procedure of many other interrogators. That became especially clear to me when I participated in questioning the four prisoners we had rolled up in the Haddoushi raid. One of them in particular caught my attention. He was a former general in the Republican Guard and was well connected to the Haddoushi clan. He was definitely someone I wanted to spend some time with. But I had a problem. After the all-day Haddoushi roundup, Adam, the terp, was burned out. He needed a break and without a terp, I was useless.

Jeff had a solution. He told me to use Allen, who was still waiting around to go back to Baghdad after the accidental discharge incident. I tried to hide my reluctance. Aside from the fact that I just didn't like the guy, I also knew that having an interrogator as an interpreter was asking for trouble. In an interrogation only one person can be in charge. When I worked with Jeff, he operated in a supervising role and the questions he asked were always in line with the direction I chose. With another interrogator, especially someone like Allen, the chances increased that the lines of authority would blur. The prisoner could take advantage of the situation.

To head off that possibility, I took Allen aside before we got started interrogating the captured general. I tried to explain the way I would be handling the questioning, based on the techniques I had learned over the past couple of weeks.

"I like to go into lots of detail," I explained. "It may not seem important at first. And you may not know where I'm going. But just bear with me."

"Sure thing," he replied with a smirk.

The session started out smoothly enough. Allen translated the questions and answers without adding or omitting anything. The prisoner was doing a good job, too—a good job lying through his teeth about any connection he might have had with Little Saddam. I was patient, without letting on that I was aware of his deception. In every interrogation, I start with the assumption that I don't know anything about the prisoner, that I have no idea what he might or might not be willing to discuss. So I just ask him about his life, the seemingly random details of his background. In my training, this was called building a timeline. The goal was to construct a chronological account of every aspect of his past: his family, his career, his finances, even his personal preferences. You were taught to either do it starting at the beginning and moving forward or picking up from the date of his capture and moving backward.

We were taught to build these timelines in sequence, but I didn't like to do it that way. I would jump around, from one period to the next and from one subject to the other. I'd ask him what job he had in 1986, and then skip to the weddings he'd recently attended. I want to know the type of car he drove twenty years ago and what he had fed his dog six days ago. The point was to keep him from guessing where I was heading. That was the only way to stop him from getting there ahead of me. I'd be all over the map, scattering the individual timeline questions throughout the interrogation. It got very confusing—for the prisoner, for the terp and for almost anyone else who watched it unfold.

But it wasn't confusing for me. I had learned to take every fragment of information I received and drop it into place on the appropriate timeline. If I found some area of discrepancy, a missed stitch in a web of lies, I'd store that away, too. I never asked a detainee to clarify a potential lie. I didn't want him to suspect that I might have caught him in a deception. Confusion was my ally. As long as the prisoner couldn't anticipate the next question, he wouldn't be able to conceal what he didn't want me to know. Then, when the time is right, I'd drop the hammer.

In some areas, I'm pretty inept. I'm not good at directions and frequently get lost as a result. I don't handle tools very well, and couldn't change a flat tire to save my life. But as an interrogator, I have the ability to remember everything a prisoner tells me, place it where it belongs, and create a mental picture. When that picture is complete, no matter how long it may take, I can see the lies standing out in sharp contrast.

Not every interrogator has that ability. Allen, for instance, started rolling his eyes impatiently after about three hours of my seemingly random questions. "You're mixing this guy up," he told me when we took a break. "You could have had a timeline two hours ago, but you keep jumping around. He can't even remember what he told you to begin with."

I looked him in the eye. "Don't worry about it," I said. "You're doing a great job translating. Just keep it up."

"No way," he replied. "This is a waste of time. Get yourself another terp."

I followed his advice and suspended the interrogation until

Adam was rested. If this guy didn't like the way I handled an interrogation, I must be doing something right.

★ ★ ★

A few days after Allen left Tikrit, the task force reeled in a big catch. His name was Rashid Abdullah and he was one of two top inner-circle bodyguards. He was a Marafiq, which meant he commanded the most elite Hamaya, those charged with personally protecting Saddam. Along with Rashid, the raid had rolled up two of his brothers and several of his sons and nephews.

"Listen, Eric," Jack said, as the detainees were brought in for interrogation. "These guys are responsible for the deaths of a lot of our men. They're bad dudes. Don't let them talk their way out of here."

This was another area where I differed from other interrogators. I really didn't care how bad a prisoner was, or was supposed to be. Maybe they'd killed Americans, but they were soldiers and that was their job. Just like our job was to kill them. Did that make us bad guys?

As far as I was concerned it was my responsibility to look at the war and the men who fought it on both sides as objectively as I could. I couldn't afford to be motivated by real emotion. I knew that when a soldier died, his family and friends would mourn for him better and longer than I ever could. I needed to focus all my attention on interrogating. I couldn't afford to take what they may or may not have done personally.

The only thing that really did light my fuse was when a prisoner lied to me. That was preventing me from doing my job. I had zero patience for that.

My assignment in this case was to question one of Rashid's

captured brothers. The guy was totally relaxed and confident from the start. He seemed to be humoring me by answering my questions and for the time being I let him. I would have plenty of opportunity to run any number of intimidating approaches, including what interrogators call a "Fear Up Harsh," when I'd inform a prisoner how much trouble he is in, at the top of my lungs. But there was no hurry. I wanted to see where he would take me on his own.

It wasn't far. After three hours, all I'd gotten him to admit was that his brother actually was a Marafiq. He had used his influence to get a good education for his children, one of whom was a medical student. Aside from traveling to Baghdad a few times, Rashid had been living peacefully at home since the war began.

That didn't add up. Rashid was an inner-circle bodyguard. His brother had insisted that he had been living unnoticed in Tikrit all this time. He'd even headed up an anti-graffiti effort in the neighborhood. How could that have happened? Wasn't he truly one of "the bad guys"?

Although it hadn't yielded any actionable intelligence, my interrogation of Rashid's brother underscored a valuable lesson. The rules of the game had changed. In terms of the power structure, Iraq was a completely different place than it had been before the war. Rashid had been directly responsible for the security and safety of Saddam. It stood to reason that he would continue to serve that function now. Instead he was sitting at home like a respectable citizen, with no involvement in the insurgency. At least that's what his brother claimed, and I believed him. All the details of his story checked out. But more important, it was clear that he wasn't trying to get on my good side by telling me what I wanted to hear. Sometimes, in an interrogation room, honesty hits you like a brick and I had just been floored by his honesty.

What mattered now was not who had once been in charge. The regime had been turned upside down and there was a whole new cast of players. To catch them, it would no longer work simply to follow the old chain of command. It didn't exist anymore. Instead I needed to listen to what the detainees and informants were telling me. Clues to piecing together the new power structure, what was happening in the street in real time, could only come from them.

There were bad guys out there for sure. We heard their incoming mortars and sniper fire every night. But maybe we didn't really know who they were.

★ ★ ★

By early September I was interrogating on a continuous basis. My workday usually started at 1300 and continued until 0200 or later. I had a full range of detainees, usually those who were suspected of either having been involved in or were planning an attack on U.S. forces. But regardless of what they had been brought in for, the techniques I used, and the thinking behind them, were the same.

More often than not there was a lack of hard evidence to prove a prisoner was involved in the insurgency. For that reason, most of them didn't believe that they were going to prison, just because they'd been arrested. It was my job to catch them in a lie if I could. That gave me leverage. If I could prove they were lying, they could be held indefinitely. But the reality in war was that I didn't have to make my case to a judge or jury. We weren't in the United States and my job wasn't to hand down justice. Frankly, I didn't care whether they were guilty or innocent of the crimes with which they'd been charged. Every prisoner I interrogated started out being guilty of one thing: not helping me yet. It was up to me whether they would go free. And the only way that would happen was when they proved themselves helpful.

I needed intelligence. It didn't matter to me whether I was getting it from an actual insurgent or a completely innocent detainee who happened to possess important information. There was no superior standing over my shoulder, watching my every move. There was no central database that my information was being fed into. In that guesthouse, it was strictly between the prisoner and me.

But I was also beginning to reach beyond the detainees in my search for good information. For that reason I developed a working relationship with the 4th ID's Tactical Humint Teams— the THTs. About twenty of these Tactical Human Intelligence Teams were scattered around the city. Usually consisting of raw but enthusiastic young interrogators and counterintelligence specialists, they were tasked with developing leads wherever they could find them. One THT, for instance, was posted at the front gate of the palace compound where civilians would show up with requests or complaints. Another group was stationed at the governor's office. While they rarely came up with actionable information on HVTs, the THTs could still provide a good picture of what was happening on the ground in Tikrit. Rich regularly met with them to cull their intelligence for anything useful. But he had to be careful. The last thing he wanted to do was give the task force the impression that they were chasing leads supplied by a bunch of boy scouts.

The rest of the team, especially Jeff, had absolutely no use for these guys, but I could see that they were doing all they could under difficult circumstances. Mostly National Guard reservists with limited training and no experience in intelligence gathering, the five-man THTs tried their best to sort through the informants who came in to barter or sell information. They were totally unequipped for the task. But I made a point of meeting with them and their sources when I had the chance. You never knew where a good lead might come from. Or where it might take you.

One THT in particular had been focused on gathering information about bodyguards. A young reservist from Utah, Sergeant Olsen, headed up the unit. Olsen was eager to please and had brought us a few informants that he thought were particularly promising. One of them claimed to know the leader of a local insurgent cell. His name was Farris Yasin Omar Al-Muslit.

That rang a bell. I remembered back to my interrogation with Taha, the chubby, sweaty detainee. He had tipped me to the link between Saddam's servant and Muhammad Haddoushi's driver. But there was something else about that session that I recalled now. Taha's brother was named Farris Yasin. He was another in the long line of Al-Muslits who kept popping up on the radar.

"Who does Farris Yasin work with?" I asked Sergeant Olsen's source.

"He has a group in the north," he replied. "It is about twenty kilometers from Al-Alam, which is my village."

I knew Al-Alam, at least by reputation. It was across the Tigris River from Tikrit and was surrounded by rich farmland awarded to key Saddam supporters. It was increasingly clear that Al-Alam and other towns on the east side of the river were hotbeds of insurgency. Most of the detainees that were brought to me were from Tikrit. As inadequate as they were, THTs like Sergeant Olsen's were some of my few links to what might be going on east of the river.

I wasn't sure where all this was leading, but I wanted to follow it as far as I could. Unfortunately Jeff's short fuse had already burned down. "Okay," he said after the session. "Where exactly did that get us?"

He had a point. We had some vague indications of an insurgent group working in an area where we rarely netted prisoners. But I didn't want to let it go yet.

"It might be good to talk to people from the other side of the river," I suggested.

"Then check with Chris," Jeff snapped back. "He runs sources out of there. You can sit in on his meetings."

The fact was that, under Chris, the case officer, we already had informants in Al-Alam and elsewhere. What we didn't have was a system for sharing the information he pulled in. I didn't know what he was doing and vice versa. We were improvising, doing the best we could with a patchwork of sources and prisoners. What we needed was to pool what we were getting, identify areas of overlap, and begin to build a broader picture of the activities and main players in the region. Jeff brought Chris and me together and decided that we would sit in on each other's interrogations and informant debriefings whenever possible. Slowly but surely, a coordinated effort was beginning to take shape.

But progress was agonizingly slow. Even with our improved information sharing, the quality of intelligence we were getting was consistently poor. In the month of September alone, the team went out on something like a half dozen hits just looking for Muhammad Haddoushi. They were all dry holes. There were another half dozen strikeouts for other assorted targets and at least ten raids that failed to turn up Izzat Ibrahim Al-Duri, Saddam's senior military adviser, the King of Clubs on the deck of cards, Black List #6.

If Al-Duri weren't still at large and suspected to be hiding somewhere in the Tikrit area, I'm not even sure that the team would still have been stationed there. He was the kind of HVT that attracted a lot of attention and there was a real premium put on rolling him up: to be exact, a $10 million bounty for information leading to his arrest. It sometimes seemed that everything else we were doing short of finding Al-Duri was just to keep us in town. We were still going on hits and collecting information, but the focus was on finding this one card in the Black List deck.

But when it came to capturing him, or any other targets, High Value or otherwise, we kept coming up short. The team blamed the intelligence collectors for the frustrating lack of success. I took my share of the blame for the lack of good information, even though their expectations of me weren't very high to begin with. But in their own way, guys like Chris were as dedicated as the shooters. They never gave up, even when, time after time, the results were discouraging.

★ ★ ★

While I now felt comfortable sharing the food in the kitchen, I drew the line at the beer stashed in the refrigerator. The shooters would bring in a couple of cases when they went to Baghdad, but I always assumed it was off-limits. They rationed themselves pretty carefully, and I never saw any of them drink more than a beer a night. They never knew when they might be called out on a hit.

It was all the more significant then when, after a grueling twelve-hour interrogation, Jeff offered me a cold beer. Jeff was a hard man to know. He stood out even among this group of men who kept to themselves and never showed what they were feeling. The fact that he offered me a beer was a major act of friendship. After that we regularly shared a cold one after a long day of work.

There was another break from my routine when football season started. The 2003 college football season was a time of high hopes for all true Sooners. We were coming in ranked number one in the polls and, over the last three years had lost only four games and won a national championship. As far as I was concerned, it wasn't a matter of whether we were going to win the national championship, but by what margin.

In Iraq the Armed Forces Network would broadcast the games on Saturday evening, starting around 1900 and usually run all night. OU was so good that year that I expected most of the games to be aired. My goal was to finish all my interrogations in time for the first kickoff.

But it didn't always work out that way. In the first week of September, the Sooners had a bye week and the Texas Longhorns, the Sooners' archrival, were playing the Arkansas Razorbacks. I had been eagerly anticipating the game and by 1500 I was on my last interrogation. I was going to be in front of the TV set no matter what.

It was then that the war intervened. Rich arrived at the guesthouse with news that the Iraqi police had arrested Nasir Yasin Omar Al-Muslit. I knew only too well who the new prisoner was. Aside from being still another Al-Muslit, Nasir was an inner-circle bodyguard. He was reputed to be one of the last people seen with Saddam at the start of the war. He was also, of course, well connected within the Hamaya chain of command. He was the brother of Farris Yasin, who was supposedly running the insurgency group around Al-Alam and was the cousin of several other high-ranking Al-Muslits.

I knew I needed to talk to him, but I was hoping it could wait. The game was about to begin. By the time Rich got through in-processing him, it would be too late to start an interrogation. Maybe this could wait until tomorrow.

No such luck. The processing procedure was going to be delayed. He would be shipped to BIAP shortly. We had to talk to him right away. Swearing under my breath, I settled in for a long night of work.

Nasir made an immediate impression. A couple of inches under six feet, he easily weighed two hundred fifty pounds and had been roughed up pretty badly by the Iraqi cops who had arrested him. But he didn't seem intimidated by the situation and showed no fear or the slightest trace of nerves. My first impression was that getting anything from this guy was going to be a chore.

It was. For the first several hours, he had his story and he stuck to it: He claimed he had no contact with his extended family and friends and was living peacefully at home with his wife and kids since the war began. I did everything I could think of to shake his self-confidence, but he wouldn't break. Finally, with Adam the terp getting hoarse from echoing my yelling and screaming, we took a break. I went back to the house to get something to eat. A group had gathered around the television. The game was in the last five minutes and Texas was getting their asses kicked. Go Razorbacks!

The prospect of the Sooners' mortal enemies getting trounced provided fresh motivation. I knew Nasir could give me invaluable information on the inner workings of the Hamaya. I just didn't know how to get it out of him. I returned to the guesthouse and started again, this time asking general questions about his life and his job. I was fishing for something, anything, that might point me in the right direction.

Slowly, over the course of the next few hours, the prisoner began to open up. Obviously he wasn't going to tell us where we might find any of his family members who were still in hiding or overseeing the insurgency. But the details of his everyday life were not out of bounds. Answering simple questions would give him the appearance of being honest and innocent and doing his best to cooperate.

What Nasir confided was a blueprint to the operation of Saddam's bodyguards. At any given time, he explained, there were thirty-two inner-circle Hamaya, divided into two sixteen-man teams on separate shifts. Each team had a leader—the Marafiq—and he provided me with their names. He also gave me the names of twenty-nine of the thirty-two inner-circle body-guards along with their ranks. It was interesting to note that rank didn't necessarily convey power within the inner circle. Rank was based solely on time of service. Power was about family con-nections and proximity to Saddam, and a major with good con-nections could carry more authority than a full-bird colonel.

I may have missed an important game, but at the end of my session with Nasir, I had learned two crucial things. First, we finally had a way into the inner circle of Hamaya, the ones most trusted by Saddam. It was no longer about an endless fra-ternity of relatives popping up at random intervals. Since my ar-rival, I had been working off the list of two hundred bodyguards of varying importance that Jared had given me. I could now concentrate on just thirty-two of them. While I still wasn't sure where those thirty-two might eventually take me, at least it was a manageable number.

The other important takeaway was that it wasn't always nec-essary to break a prisoner in order to get good information. I was never able to frighten or intimidate Nasir into telling me what I wanted to know. But just by talking with him about his life as a bodyguard, I learned more than I had from a dozen other interrogations. The fact was, Nasir was a prime example of a prisoner whose guilt or innocence didn't really matter. I was in the business of getting information and it didn't matter if the source was good, bad, or indifferent, as long as he had what I needed. And I could find a way to get it out of him

☆ ☆ ☆

It was shortly after OU whipped UCLA in late September that Sergeant Olsen approached me again about some other sources he had been developing.

This time it was a trio of guys who lived east of the Tigris not far from Al-Alam. Olsen called them the Three Amigos. He wanted me to talk to them because they claimed to have knowledge about the Al-Muslits, specifically Radman Ibrahim.

Radman was the cousin of Nezham, whom we'd been after on the raid the night I first arrived in Tikrit. I'd since found out that Radman had been an administrator for the inner circle of Hamaya and was considered one of the most powerful members of the bodyguard elite. Olsen's three sources claimed that this high-ranking Al-Muslit still occasionally visited a farm he owned in the area north of Tikrit. They were offering their services to let us know the next time he showed up.

"Why are you willing to help us capture him?" I asked them after they'd been brought over to the guesthouse.

"We want to work for the governor of Tikrit," the self-appointed spokesman replied. "Maybe you will put in a good word for us." The fact was, these three didn't really have much of a connection to Radman. All they had was a vague idea of his whereabouts and his role in the insurgency. But at least their enthusiasm counted for something.

"But we will need vehicles, weapons, and telephones to do the job," added another amigo.

"What for?"

"When we have a car we will join the insurgency," the spokesman explained. "We will protect ourselves with weapons. And when we find Radman, we will call and tell you."

I stifled a laugh. "Let's get this straight," I said. "You help me get a bad guy and maybe I can help you. But not until then. In the meantime, find out what you can about Radman and let me know when you get something we can use."

They didn't like it, but they didn't have a choice. We agreed to meet again in ten days to see if they had found out anything. I had my doubts.

But I did have the feeling that things were beginning to move, even though I had no idea where they were going or how to get out ahead of them. Working with the THT sources hadn't produced much in the way of results, but neither had most of my interrogations. I was still looking for patterns, networks, or a string of simple coincidences that might add up and get us somewhere. The Three Amigos would probably produce nothing, but I couldn't afford to ignore any possibility, no matter how slim.

Through constant interrogating, I was slowly beginning to get a better picture of insurgency activities in Tikrit itself. Some of it was being conducted by young Iraqi men who had formed loose-knit gangs to kill Americans. There was little difference between them and any Crip or Blood in a U.S. inner city. The ones who actually did the shooting or set off the IEDs became the leaders, while others joined purely because of peer pressure.

One of the most notorious of these gangsters was a kid named Munthir. He controlled three small but deadly insurgency cells. In late September, his house was raided. Munthir wasn't there, but four of his brothers were captured and brought in for interrogation. The information they provided was of limited usefulness. But the hunt for Munthir did provide me with an important new source of intelligence about what was happening on the streets of Tikrit.

We called this new source Fred. He had been working with Chris as one of his informants and had given him Munthir's supposed location. As a street criminal, he was adept at infiltrating these teenage insurgency groups. When Chris finished debriefing him, I began talking with him as well. He was a fountain of information, providing details about specific neighborhoods in Tikrit, who operated where, and whether they were part of a bigger organization.

But I still needed to find a way to bring it all together, to link the suspects and sources and separate players. Maybe it was all nothing more than a freelance network of insurgents working on their own. But maybe not. Maybe someone was running the whole thing.

CHAPTER 8

CHANGING THE GUARD

1945 11OCT2003

By early October, the team's tour of duty in Tikrit was coming to an end. As they prepared to leave, I naturally thought back over the last nine weeks. Even though you couldn't call it a full-on success, I still felt that we had accomplished a lot. We had captured several bad guys and helped to identify dozens of others. We had helped to maintain a strong American presence in a part of the country that had been intensely loyal to Saddam. Most importantly, we were beginning to make progress in unraveling Tikrit's network of power and influence.

I was sorry to see the team go. I had gotten as close to them as they would allow anyone to come. It was an honor to have served with such a group of elite soldiers. I was especially going to miss Jeff. Without question, he was a hard man to deal with. But he had also given me a lot of freedom to sharpen my interrogation skills and follow the leads I uncovered wherever they took me. In addition to hundreds of interrogations, I had sat in on upwards of thirty source meetings. Despite the fact that the raids only occasionally rolled up the targets we were after, Jeff still understood the value of a good interrogator, no matter how time-consuming the process was. The same was true of Rich, the analyst, and Chris, the case officer. We'd worked well together.

I had no idea whether the new team would be as willing to let me do my job with the same freedom. I didn't even know if they would want me to stay in Tikrit. It was going to be like starting from scratch, but with one important difference: I would be the one person who could tell them what was happening on the ground in the town. It was going to take time for the new team to get up to speed. I had suddenly become the resident expert.

Not that I had any clear strategy. I was still trying to fit the puzzle together and it was a painstaking process. Yet, even by the end of September, the pieces of the puzzle had started to come together. We were focusing on several likely suspects who might actually be aiding and abetting the insurgency in the Tikrit area. High on that list were men like Radman Ibrahim, Farris Yasin, and Haddoushi, although conclusive evidence against them was hard to come by. I actually had my own theory as to why Haddoushi was still a high priority: It was his name. It was fun to say. I had once overhead a guard at the 4th ID prison calling his buddy on a radio by saying, "Hey, Haddoushi get over here." In another incidence, one sentry called to another: "Cover this gate. I got to take a Haddoushi." It had a certain ring to it. My theory was almost too ridiculous to tell anyone, but I was certain it was true.

We had also filled in a lot of the Al-Muslit family tree. There were, in all, some forty Al-Muslit men of fighting age in Tikrit. We knew who they were, where they lived before the war, and their place in the family hierarchy. Most of them had served, or had been in line to serve, in the Hamaya. Why this family? Why were so many of them bodyguards? Those were the questions I was still trying to answer as the team packed their bags.

It was the day of the OU–Texas game at the Cotton Bowl, the Sooners biggest game of the year. The last members of the old unit had left and their replacements were on the way. I exchanged a few brief but heartfelt good-byes with the departing soldiers. Within a few days, Tikrit would be a memory for them. For me it was still a reality, a place that exhausted all my energy and attention.

Ten minutes before kickoff, word came that the new shooters had arrived. We went out to the airfield to greet them and help them unload. As badly as I wanted to see that game, I also knew I didn't want to be the dirtbag sitting around watching TV when the new guys showed up. On the ride back to the house, I met some of the new operators, answering their standard questions about the food and accommodations. I noticed that they were younger than the previous team: an operator named Jeremy looked like he was pulling weekend duty for the Junior ROTC. But they were the same superbly trained warriors as those they had replaced, and there was no doubt about their professionalism and determination. The team was balanced with a few older guys, too. Scott had been in the Army for eighteen years. Doug, the sergeant major who took Matt's place, was also a career soldier and well respected by his men. John was team commander, but everyone called him "Bam Bam." I never did find out exactly why. He was quiet and conscientious, and he turned out to be one of the smartest officers I'd ever worked for.

By the time we got back to the house, the Sooners were dismantling Texas, 35–7. But I still didn't get a chance to sit down and watch the game. For the next couple of hours I showed the arrivals around their new quarters. After that, the new intelligence analyst, Kelly, wanted to talk with me.

"Before he left," Kelly said, "Rich took me to a lot of places and introduced me to a lot of people. But I still really don't know where we are in the fight."

"Ask me anything."

"Okay. Where is Saddam?"

"He could be in Tikrit." I was interested in how Kelly might react to that statement.

"Do you really believe that?" He seemed surprised. I was surprised myself. It was the first time I'd ever shared with anyone the conclusion I had begun to draw. In fact, I wasn't sure I *did* believe it. But I wasn't sure I didn't, either.

"Is Black List number six, Al-Duri with him?"

I took a deep breath. This was my time to test the waters with my Saddam theory. This guy didn't know what had been going on here the last three months. There wasn't anyone left here to tell him except me. I could pitch this any way I wanted. "We're not interested in Al-Duri," I told him in a confidential tone. "He's no longer a player. We've got other players we're after now."

"Like who?"

Over the next forty-five minutes I gave Kelly a full data dump. It was then, for the first time, I spelled out in detail the hypotheses that had been coming together for me over the last few weeks. "Saddam trusted his bodyguards," I explained. "We know that. We also know that there were thirty-two of them in the inner circle. We've identified them all. Some were killed and captured. Some have left the country. And there are some still here in Tikrit."

"How many?"

"There are probably ten leaders of the entire insurgency here. I think four of them are from the Al-Muslit tribe. All of them were inner-circle Hamaya. They were linked directly to Saddam. Maybe they still are."

"Where are the reports on this?" Kelly asked.

"I've got it all in my head."

He glanced around the room where we were sitting, the one Rich had used as his office. Pinned on the walls were link diagrams with names in boxes connected by lines of influence and family ties. "Is that what you're talking about?" he asked.

I shook my head. "Those have been here since before the last group came. None of the people I'm looking for are on those diagrams."

"Well, put up your own then," he said. "Get all these diagrams down on paper. I need to get up to speed on this. If you die and it's all still in your head, we'll have to start over."

✯ ✯ ✯

I could have gone a lot further with Kelly that night. But I didn't want to overload him. What I had told him was a general overview, but I had already narrowed my focus from the list of thirty-two inner-circle bodyguards Nasir had given me. Through countless hours of interrogation, chasing down numerous rabbit holes, I finally zeroed in on four specific Al-Muslits: the brothers Radman Ibrahim, Muhammad Ibrahim, and Khalil Ibrahim, along with their cousin Farris Yasin. These were the names that kept coming up in talking with detainees and informants. The four had taken an increasingly central place in the link diagrams I had created in my mind, connected to numerous former regime members, Hamaya, and known insurgents. As I'd sifted though hundreds of pages of my notes, I could make out the faint traces of a pattern that kept taking me back to these four men.

But there were still a lot of questions to be answered. Why

would the Al-Muslits be involved in the insurgency at all? Most of them had been men of position and rank. They didn't need money: Saddam had seen to that. The only motive that made any sense was personal loyalty to their leader. These men had been sworn to protect and obey Saddam. Whom could he trust now, if he was in hiding or on the run?

The truth was, I was a lot more convinced that Saddam was somewhere in or around Tikrit than I had let on to Kelly. My evidence was the close proximity of bodyguards in the area, particularly the Al-Muslit brothers and their cousin. Saddam would keep them close. They might still be following his orders.

I wasn't sure whether I'd made a convincing case to Kelly, but over the next few days I had the opportunity to present my theory again. This time it was to the team's commander, Bam Bam, as well as to Rod, the new case officer who had replaced Chris. In his early thirties and a former Special Operations soldier, Rod had a great attitude. He was willing to accept that he didn't know anything about the situation and was willing to learn from anyone who did. I became his primary source of information.

At first it was a little overwhelming for him. Rod tried to write down as much as he could, putting it on a white memo board and hanging it on his wall. He had listed the names of the primary targets I'd provided, along with a brief description of what was known about them.

One particular entry on that white board reflected both the extent of my knowledge and my ignorance of the insurgency network in Tikrit. The name was Muhammad Ibrahim, one of the three Al-Muslit brothers I had identified as prime suspects. Next to it Rod had written "Wildcard." That pretty much summed it up. The intelligence I'd gathered often referred to Muhammad

Ibrahim as the primary insurgent leader. But none of the prisoners or sources had allegedly spoken to him or even seen him since before the war. If he was in any way still connected to the bodyguard brotherhood, he was doing a great job of keeping a low profile.

The same wasn't true of his brother Radman. Although he was just as elusive, we occasionally got word of his whereabouts and activities. The Three Amigos, the walk-in sources brought to me by Sergeant Olsen, claimed they could hunt him down. So did two Kurds, who had worked as informants for Chris shortly before he left. In early October they came to us claiming that Radman was way out west in the city of Haditha. If we raided the location within the next three hours, we'd capture him. That wasn't possible. We'd need at least twelve hours to properly prepare for the hit. The Kurds were clearly disappointed, but promised to come back when they could provide a larger window for Radman's whereabouts. I really liked their motivation. There was no hidden agenda. As Kurds, a persecuted minority under the regime, they hated Saddam. It was as simple as that.

As Rod settled into his new job, he began working more closely with Fred, the young street criminal who was our best source for the teenage gangs that served as foot soldiers for the insurgency. Unlike the Kurds, Fred had a mixed motive for his cooperation. He had aspirations to be the leader of his tribe and encouraged us to arrest any and all of his rivals for the position. He had also developed a crush on Zita, a local female translator who had volunteered to help us. He never came to a session without a gift for her.

Yet we all agreed that it took a criminal to catch a criminal. Rod directed most of Fred's efforts toward keeping tabs on

Munthir, the most notorious of the gang leaders. But it was gratifying when Rod subsequently approached me to double-check
the list of targets I had identified. I had reason to hope that he
would direct Fred to keep a lookout for the Al-Muslit brothers
and their cousin Farris Yasin.

The frequency of hits dropped sharply in the first week following the team's arrival. They were getting familiar with their
new surroundings. But they were also waiting for the intelligence staff to provide them with concrete targets. I had made as
good a case as I could for the Al-Muslit connection to Saddam
and their involvement in the insurgency, but I still had no hard
evidence to back up my claims. Rod asked more than once why
we were after guys that he'd never heard of. I needed to give him
a reason.

I finally got one when I interrogated Ahmed Yasin, yet another of the nine brothers who made up the Al-Muslit fraternity.
Ahmed wasn't on my list of key Al-Muslit targets simply because
his name hadn't come up during interrogations or source meetings. But that didn't mean he wasn't worth interrogating. One
of the most important lessons I had learned during the last two
months was that completely innocent people could provide important information about extremely guilty people.

No more than twenty years old, Ahmed, the overweight kid
brother in the family, had been picked up by the local police a
week earlier. He'd been held for four days before being trans-
ferred to the 4th ID.

After six hours of fruitless questioning he finally started
to break. "What is your involvement with the insurgency?" I
asked.

"I already told the other interrogators everything I knew."

I looked around. "Do you see those guys here?"

He shook his head.

"That's because they're not here. I don't care what you told them. I only care what you tell me. So let's start from the beginning."

Ahmed had already admitted to some low-level involvement in the insurgency. He had even taken soldiers on a raid of his uncle's house, although it had turned out to be a dry hole. But I wasn't interested in that. I wanted to know about his brothers. And I was willing to go all night to get what I wanted.

"The men you are involved with are very bad, Ahmed," I told him. "They have killed many Americans and innocent Iraqis."

"I did not want to get involved," he pleaded, his jowls quivering. "I was so happy to be captured. That is why I am trying to help the Americans."

"You're full of shit. You've been with the insurgency from the start."

"No mister. They made me join. They told me I had to when my brother Nasir was arrested. He delivered weapons. And they made me do it in his place."

Nasir Yasin Omar Al-Muslit. Another senior bodyguard and another Al-Muslit. Ahmed had just implicated his own brother. It was the first independent corroboration I'd had from an Al-Muslit that another Al-Muslit was directly involved in the insurgency.

There comes a point in some interrogations when you have a chance to turn it all around. When that happens, you can't think about your next move. You can't reveal to the prisoner what's at stake with the next question. You have to take your shot before he fully realizes what he's just said.

"Listen to me, asshole. Who was Nasir delivering weapons

for? Lie to me and you'll never get out of this prison. You'll die here."

The kid was shaking. "I don't know," he whined. "Nasir told me Radman was involved."

I sat back in my chair. It was unexpected but gratifying. My theory was proving itself true. Now at last I had a direct link to one of the four Al-Muslits I had put on the top of my most wanted list. But I was just getting started.

"Does Nasir work directly for Radman?"

"No. He gets messages from Farris."

Farris Yasin Omar Al-Muslit? This was another of Ahmed's brothers and one of my top four Al-Muslit suspects. It was confirmation of everything I had told Kelly, Bam Bam, and Rod, even though I hadn't quite believed it myself before now.

"Is Farris higher than Radman?"

Ahmed shook his head. "Farris plans attacks and has two groups. But he's not a big leader."

"Who is the big leader? Is it Radman?"

"I don't know. I never see Radman."

"Do you see Farris? Don't lie to me."

He thought for a moment. "Farris has two friends," he finally said. "They are Shakir and Abu Qasar. They would know where he is. They are very close."

"Are they in the insurgency?"

"Shakir, maybe," he answered. "But Abu Qasar is too old. He just sits all day and plays dominoes."

I made a mental note of the names, than turned to my next area of interest. "What about Radman's brother, your uncle Muhammad Ibrahim? Have you seen him?"

"Maybe two weeks ago," he replied. "He was driving through Tikrit. I am certain it was him."

"Who does Muhammad Ibrahim report to?"

"Mister, Muhammad Ibrahim he does not report to anyone. Except the president."

For one of the first times in my life I was left speechless. The president was Saddam.

CHAPTER 9

NINETY PERCENT

1100 14OCT2003

My interrogation with Ahmed had been a gold mine. I made sure to tell Kelly exactly what I had found out. He quickly passed the news on Bam Bam and Rod.

"I'm told you have the entire Tikrit network mapped out in your head," Bam Bam said to me the next morning at the dining room table. "Is that true?"

"Yes, sir," I replied.

"You need to make sure you and Kelly get a link diagram done," he told me. "And quit calling me, sir. Call me Bam Bam. Everyone else does."

I obeyed both orders and by that night had put together a chart with about sixty names on it. They were broken out into tiers according to my best estimate of each suspect's importance in the insurgency.

At the top, of course, was Saddam. Below him were the Al-Muslit brothers and Muhammad Haddoushi. Kelly also insisted on adding Al-Duri. I didn't object; even though it seemed like a waste of time, I realized he was a priority for the others. But

I knew who belonged at the top of that chart. The only targets I wanted the new team to focus on were the Al-Muslits. From Ahmed Yasin's interrogation on, I would ignore any rumors or tips on Al-Duri that might come my way.

I also wanted to drop Haddoushi from the list, even though he remained a number one priority for the 4th ID. I'd been chasing this guy since I got to Tikrit and was beginning to have my doubts about his value as a target. The reason he had been singled out was because his nephew had been killed in the shoot-out with Saddam's sons, Uday and Qusay. The assumption was that because they were involved, so was he. But as time went on I was less and less convinced that Haddoushi was active in the insurgency, much less that he could take us to Saddam.

To my way of thinking, I wasn't being prejudicial in the preferences for the link diagram, just selective. I was still talking to dozens of people a week, from low-level detainees to walk-ins to sources. The questioning, in turn, produced hundreds of names of people who might or might not have been worth pursuing. Some of them, no doubt, were bad guys. Others may have been totally innocent or an enemy someone wanted us to get out of the way. It was my job to sort through it all and select targets whose capture would decapitate the insurgency. I had already decided who those targets were.

When Kelly and I finished the link diagram, he warned me to keep it out of sight if any top brass should drop by for a visit. The priorities I had established were definitely not the same ones being worked everywhere else in Iraq. What was important to me was that Kelly and Bam Bam didn't reject them outright. Kelly just didn't want anyone else to know what we were doing. It was a legitimate concern. We might get shut down before we got started.

I was in a unique position. When I'd first arrived in Tikrit, I had no say in the targets we went after. They had been established before I got there. But in the months that followed, as the raids kept producing dry holes, it was clear our intelligence capabilities were coming up short. We needed a new approach and I was in the right place at the right time to provide it.

Yet even with the arrival of the new team, I didn't have the authority or influence to take the hunt where I thought it should go. I was still just one link in an intelligence-gathering team that weighed and evaluated information from many sources. The information gathered from prisoners was still considered of less value than what came from the sources developed by case officers.

That situation changed one afternoon in late October. Rod, the case officer who had arrived with the new team, was a former Navy SEAL. He occasionally joined the operators at the shooting range; it was as much to try to establish a rapport with the elite soldiers as to hone his own skills. But something had gone wrong and he'd been wounded by a stray fragment from an M-203. An M-203 is a grenade launcher that attaches to the bottom of an M-4 rifle, and under normal circumstances should have exploded a safe distance from the shooter. The freak accident had sent a small piece of shrapnel into Rod's stomach and, although the wound wasn't serious, they couldn't locate the piece and would have to perform exploratory surgery. He was immediately out of commission and was shipped off to Germany for medical treatment.

I liked Rod. We'd had the beginnings of a good working relationship and I was sorry to see him go. On the other hand, the accident presented me with a chance to organize our intelligence operation in a whole new way. By the next day, I had been informed that Rod was not going to be replaced. I was being handed his sources and was to guide them as I saw fit. Rod's boss was going to handle all the logistics with the sources, but it was up to me now to decide which targets they would go after. Rod's misfortune had been a stroke of luck for me. I was suddenly in charge of all human intelligence for the team. Along with interrogating, I would now be running the source meetings. It no longer mattered whether it was from prisoners or informants. There would finally be a coordinated effort to gather actionable intelligence in Tikrit.

And I already knew exactly how I wanted to focus the new resources. I didn't waste any time. Meeting with my old friend Sergeant Olsen, who commanded one of the most conscientious of the 4th ID's THT teams, I debriefed him on everything I had learned about the Al-Muslits. The implication was clear: these were the guys we were going after now. Olsen returned the next day with the Three Amigos in tow. I hadn't talked to the trio of informants since I'd sent them off a few weeks earlier to see if they could find Radman. Now they were back, claiming they had a lead on Farris Yasin instead. They still wanted weapons, vehicles, and cell phones. I wasn't sure about these guys but still thought they might be useful.

"Farris Yasin has two friends," I told them, recalling what Ahmed had revealed. "One of them is Shakir and the other is Abu Qasar. Where are they?"

"Shakir is the leader of an insurgency group in the north," the spokesman replied.

"What about Abu Qasar?"

They looked at each other, grinning. "Mister," the main amigo continued, "you can find Abu Qasar yourself. He is always at the teashop in town. He is too old to fight."

"Is he a friend of Farris Yasin?"

They all nodded.

"So go get him."

"We will soon get you Farris Yasin," the spokesman insisted. "Abu Qasar is nothing."

"Good," I replied. "Then you shouldn't have a problem bringing him to me. You do that and I'll give each of you an AK-47. Hell, I'll even throw in a car."

✴ ✴ ✴

It wasn't until early November that we finally got a break in the search for the top tier of Al-Muslits. The problem was, I didn't recognize it when it finally showed up.

The information had come from a source that the 4th ID military police had been developing. His name was Izzecki, from the northern city of Kirkuk, and he was in his early twenties. He'd been brought to me in the first place because he insisted that he knew exactly where Farris Yasin was and would take us to him immediately. But I had the feeling that something wasn't lining up with the kid. He claimed to be Farris Yasin's best friend. That seemed unlikely since there was at least a thirty-year age difference between them. He also couldn't tell me much about the family or prewar activities of this powerful Al-Muslit. Then he drew a blank when I asked him to name some other friends of Farris Yasin. He had no knowledge of either Shakir or the old man Abu Qasar whom I knew were close to Farris.

It was pretty much downhill from there. Izzecki insisted he had no prior knowledge of his supposed friend's insurgent activities. It was only when he learned that the Americans wanted Farris that he decided to turn him in for the reward. There would be a fight to the death, he warned, when we tried to arrest Farris. He insisted that we should bomb the house where he was hiding.

I wasn't worried about a fight to the death. I knew the team would be in and out of the location before anyone could react. What really bothered me was the fact that this kid had come out of nowhere with valuable intelligence on a dangerous insurgent leader and wanted us to hit him with everything we had. At the same time, he refused to go on the raid or to pick out Farris from a lineup if we captured him alive.

Who was really at that site? Was it Farris Yasin or someone Izzecki wanted out of the way? Maybe this was all about using the Americans to do his dirty work and pick up some quick cash in the bargain.

After a couple of hours, I took Kelly aside and recommended that we definitely not raid the house that Izzecki had identified as Farris Yasin's hideout. But the 4th ID military police battalion commander didn't see it that way. And he had the power to give the raid a green light. Behind every one of these hazardous sorties was a political reality that made them even more risky. The task force in Baghdad was keeping a close watch on everything that happened in the regions where teams had been assigned. Tikrit was no different. We had had our share of dry holes and while the difficulties of procuring actionable intelligence was understood, every one of those failed raids had a name attached to it. Get enough black marks next to your name and they'd get someone else to do your job.

But it wasn't even as simple as that. There were degrees of failure. If you raided a house in search of a target and couldn't prove he had ever been there, you got written up for a completely dry hole. If you could establish that he'd been there within the last forty-eight hours, you got away with what I called a damp hole. Not as bad. If the guy had actually been there within the last two hours but you just missed him, you'd pretty much done your job.

The worst thing that could happen was approving a hit that turned out to be an ambush. I didn't think that was what Izzecki was leading us into, but I was pretty sure it was a completely dry hole and I didn't want it in my file. I just didn't trust the guy and didn't want to take a chance on what I considered to be, at best, questionable information.

I went with Kelly to break the news to the battalion commander, a colonel with whom I'd worked before. He'd made it clear he was after big fish and believed that he had an instinctive knack for sorting good information from bad. "It just feels right," he'd say. I knew it was about more than just feeling. My gut might be telling me something, but that was never enough. I had to prove it, tie up the loose ends, and fill in the blanks. Even then, it sometimes wasn't sufficient. Men would be putting themselves in harm's way based on my best guess. I had to make sure it was as educated and objective as possible.

"Sir," I told the colonel, "there is a ninety percent chance that Farris Yasin is not going to be there."

Those were odds he was willing to take. With a hard-edged stare he told us, "I just want to make sure you realize that if you don't want it, then we'll do this hit ourselves."

We returned to the house. It was the day before the Sooners' game with Texas A&M, who had ruined our chances of an undefeated season the year before. I was more nervous about the outcome of that game than whether or not I had made the right decision about the hit: there was just no way that kid knew Farris Yasin. After another long night of interrogations, I finally crawled into bed. A few hours later, Bam Bam was shaking me by the shoulder.

"Eric," he said. "I need you to go over to the MPs and pick up Farris Yasin."

I wasn't sure whether I was dreaming. I hoped I was. Aside from recommending a raid that becomes an ambush, the second most serious screwup is turning down a solid hit. I sat up in bed with a sinking feeling in the pit of my stomach. I wasn't sure what was worse: preventing the team from capturing one of the most wanted Al-Muslits on my own list, or having to face the colonel who had actually done the job against my advice.

Kelly offered to go over with me to the 4th ID compound to pick up the prisoner. "What am I going to say to the colonel?" I wondered as we made our way through the checkpoint.

"Don't look at me," Kelly replied. "I'm not the one who told him ninety percent."

✳ ✳ ✳

From then on, things only got worse. Farris Yasin was one of the hardest and most frustrating interrogations I'd ever conducted. I knew he was a hardened criminal, a street thug, and a gang-ster. I knew he was probably responsible for the deaths of more Americans than anyone I'd interrogated in that guesthouse. And I knew he had a wealth of information about the insurgency and the men who led it. He also knew that I knew who he was and what he was doing. He had absolutely zero motivation to cooperate.

On the other hand, I was nothing but motivated. I not only wanted everything that he could tell me, I also had something to prove. I was determined to make up for the serious mistake of not recommending the raid that had brought him in. I had to break him.

But I couldn't. I realized what I was up against when, after an hour and a half, all that I'd gotten him to admit was his name. The next four hours were filled with endless repetitions of the same bullshit story: he hadn't seen any of his family since before the war; he had no involvement with the insurgency or with anyone who did; he spent his days hunting birds. He didn't blink an eye when I called him a liar and a terrorist and a shitbag or when I promised him that he'd never get out of prison while I was still alive. I got the feeling he was actually enjoying this battle of wills. It was a point of pride not to show fear or doubt or guilt.

The grinding interrogation went on all day. Trying to catch him in an inconsistency was pointless. Since he was telling me nothing to begin with, there was nothing for him to contradict. I wanted to hear about Izzecki, the kid who had turned him in, but knew better than to reveal that I had that information. Izzecki's name never came up, despite my best efforts to lead Farris Yasin in that direction. There were other questions that I couldn't ask. Who the hell was Izzecki, anyway? How did he know where Farris was? Why did he turn him in? I was convinced that the stories he had told about the insurgent leader being his best friend were lies. Nothing Farris was saying or not saying was changing my mind. But I couldn't figure out what the connection between the two men might be.

Eight hours later I had still not gotten a single piece of useful information. I even tried confronting him with the man whose house he was hiding in. He'd also been rolled up in the raid. I pointed out small discrepancies between their stories.

"He's scared," Farris said smugly. "He wants to please you. He will say whatever lies he thinks you want to hear."

At 1500 I was called out of the interrogation room. There were two men at the gate, Kelly informed me. They needed to talk to me right away.

"Who are they?" I asked. I was in no mood to deal with random walk-ins.

"Two Kurds," Kelly replied. "They're looking for you. They say you told them to come back when they found Radman Ibrahim. They're telling us he's in Hudaytha and will be there until tomorrow morning."

That got my attention. These were obviously the same two Kurds that had been working as sources with Chris before he left. They had come back now, with the intelligence I'd sent them out to get: the location of one of the top Al-Muslits and a twelve-hour window in which to launch the raid. Suddenly, my luck was changing. The exhausting day I'd just spent questioning Farris Yasin for information was now moving in a whole other direction.

"What do you think?" one of the terps asked me as we went to talk to the Kurds. "Are these guys for real?"

"I don't know if you've heard," I answered grimly, "but last night the MPs picked up Farris Yasin on a hit I turned down. If these two guys told me they *dreamed* where Radman was, I'd recommend we go."

After a thorough debriefing I was convinced that the sources were telling the truth. A consultation with Bam Bam convinced him, too and the raid was quickly put together. This was turning out to be one of the busiest and most eventful nights of my tour in Tikrit. And I wasn't even factoring in the OU–A&M game that was going on at the same time.

Two hours later, the shooters had left on the raid that would hopefully roll up Radman. I returned to Farris Yasin, this time bringing with me his young brother, Ahmed Yasin. Ahmed repeated everything he had told me earlier, especially about Farris being an active member of the insurgency, but once again the result was negligible. I wasn't getting anywhere.

But I still had hopes for the unfolding raid. Taking a well-deserved break from Farris, I returned to the house and went directly to the room the team used as an office. As I entered, Kelly, who was crouched at the radio, jumped up.

"Jackpot!" he shouted. "They got him."

"Are you sure?" I asked. At that point, I wasn't leaving anything to chance.

"That was Bam Bam," he replied, pointing to the radio. "He wouldn't call if he wasn't sure."

I let myself breathe again. "When will they be back? When can I start interrogating Radman?"

"Well," Kelly said hesitantly. "That's sort of an issue."

I didn't like the sound of that. "What do you mean an 'issue'?"

"Hudaytha is pretty far west from here," he explained. "We had to do the hit with our team in Baghdad. We drove out, but they came in on choppers. They're going to fly Radman back to BIAP with them."

My heart sank. "That's a huge mistake, Kelly," I protested. "They don't even know who he is. I don't want Radman because he's a bad guy. I want him because of what he can tell me. He can lay out the entire insurgency here in Tikrit. He might even lead us to Saddam."

"It's a logistical issue," Kelly said with a shrug. "Bam Bam's trying to get it straightened out, but they may want to keep him for a few days. I'll try to get him back here for you as soon as I can."

We were interrupted by the radio. A message was coming in from the returning team: *We have the PC.* It was shorthand for "Precious Cargo."

"What do you know," Kelly said. "I guess Bam Bam talked Baghdad into letting us have Radman after all."

I leapt up and rushed back to the guesthouse, stopping long enough to get a few No-Doze from my kit. I'd been up so long now, I knew I'd need something to help keep me alert for the interrogation with my new High Value prisoner.

When, after a half hour, nobody had showed up for the interrogation, I went out looking for the operators who would be escorting Radman. I ran into Bam Bam coming down the path.

"Did you get my message?" he asked with a slight smile.

"Yes," I said anxiously. "Where is he? I'm ready to get started."

"Oh, I was just messing with you," Bam Bam replied, his smile turning into a grin. "They took him to Baghdad. It wasn't my choice. I knew you'd be pissed."

Bam Bam had gotten me good. As I walked back to the house, deflated and discouraged, I felt the No-Doze starting to kick in. It was going to be a long and useless night.

CHAPTER 10

BABY RADMAN

0230 08NOV2003

I barely had time to catch my breath after the chain of events that had gone down in the last twenty-four hours. Two top Al-Muslits had been captured on the same day. That was the good news. But along with it came the reality that Farris Yasin was no closer to breaking than when he'd first been brought in. And Radman was now hundreds of miles away in the BIAP prison. It was frustrating to be so close to unraveling the insurgent web and yet not be able to close it out. I was still dealing with circumstances beyond my control.

But the pace was definitely picking up and I needed to stay one step ahead of it. When Kelly told me that Izzecki, the kid who had turned in Farris Yasin, was back to collect his reward, I had them bring him out to the guesthouse. I was determined to pinpoint the connection between the two of them. My hope was that something Izzecki might tell me could prove helpful in getting Farris to finally talk.

I began the way I usually did, by asking him about his family. Those links were often the most important in establishing where loyalties lay and secrets might be hidden. But there was nothing in what he told me that I could tie in with the men I was after. At least not initially.

"Tell me about your father," I prompted him.

"He was in the army for five years," Izzecki replied. "Now he has a store. A food market in our village."

"What village?"

"Al-Alam."

"Does the rest of your family live in Al-Alam?"

"My grandfather does."

"Where is your grandfather now?"

"He is here. He drove me to get my money."

"Does your grandfather have other sons?"

"I have two uncles. The youngest is named Muhammad. The oldest is Qasar."

I paused for a moment, but the gears in my head kept turning. Izzecki had an uncle named Qasar. In Arabic culture, when a man has a son, the word "Abu" is added to his name. That made Izzecki's grandfather Abu Qasar. Abu Qasar was one of the two friends of Farris Yasin, whom Ahmed had told me about.

Suddenly it all made sense. The old man knew that we were looking for him in connection with a wanted insurgent leader. I had given the Three Amigos specific instructions to bring him in. So he'd sent his grandson to turn in Farris Yasin instead and keep himself out of trouble. As the old saying goes, with friends like that, who needs enemies? Now I understood why Izzecki had been so sketchy on the details of Farris's life and family. All he knew was what his grandfather, Abu Qasar, had instructed him to say: go to the Americans and tell them where Farris Yasin is hiding.

I called in the old man and spent a few hours trying to find out what else he might know about his supposed best buddy. I was particularly interested in the whereabouts of Farris's other best friend, Shakir. But Abu Qasar pleaded ignorance and there wasn't much point in trying to prove otherwise. The only reason I'd been interested in Abu Qasar and Shakir in the first place was because of what they might have told me about Farris Yasin. Now that he was in custody, his two friends were off the hook. All I'd really wanted to figure out was how Izzecki had known of Farris's whereabouts. I had still been trying to sort out how I could have blown the hit that brought him in. Now I had my answer.

But there was another lesson to be learned from the Izzecki incident. Otherwise innocent individuals could provide as much valuable information as the guiltiest insurgent. Abu Qasar had known exactly where we could find Farris Yasin. All it took was some indirect pressure to crack him. The problem came in trying to apply that pressure. There was no way I could convince Kelly or Bam Bam to go after targets just because they were a friend or associate of a bad guy. We weren't supposed to be in the guilt by association business. But that's where the information was. It was becoming clear to me that Farris Yasin was never going to reveal the extent of his own or his cousin's involvement in the insurgency. Those blood ties just ran too deep. But it was amazing what otherwise upstanding citizens can tell you if you provide the right incentive.

✯ ✯ ✯

The obstacles I was facing in trying to expose the Al-Muslit's leadership of the Tikrit insurgency got a lot higher when news came from BIAP that Radman Ibrahim had died of a massive heart attack while in custody.

This was a major setback. I had focused a lot of energy and attention on Radman, based on my belief that he was a senior member of the Al-Muslit brotherhood. Now he was gone and with him a vital link in the chain of command. I'd never had a chance to interrogate him and, with Farris Yasin still refusing to cooperate, I was facing a dead end. Kelly and Bam Bam, as well as the rest of the team, were willing to hang in as long as I could show I was making progress. But after Radman's death, I was running out of viable options. I didn't know how much longer I could maintain their confidence.

Grasping at straws, I asked Kelly to arrange for Radman's son to be brought back from Baghdad. He had been captured along with his father, but the task force command was getting ready to cut him loose. He was only eighteen years old and had watched his own father die in an American jail cell. The Baghdad brass just wanted to wash their hands of the whole situation. "I think we can get him up here," Kelly told me, "but we're going to have to release him pretty soon."

"I'll take him for as long as I can get him," I replied. I figured I'd have maybe thirty-six hours and I wanted to make the most of it.

Radman's son arrived that night. His name was Awad, but I always thought of him as "Baby Radman." He was obviously scared and traumatized by what he'd been through. For me, his state of mind was a definite advantage. I could use his fear to get him talking. For that reason I came at him hard right from the beginning. After a couple of hours, I was pretty sure he wasn't actively involved in the insurgency. But that didn't mean he had nothing to tell me. Izzecki and his grandfather had taught me that.

My tactic with Baby Radman was to accuse him over and

over of knowing about his father's role in the insurgency. The one key fact I was able to exploit was his admission that his dad was hiding from coalition forces. You don't hide if you've got nothing to hide. But that only got me so far. Guilty or innocent, Radman was dead. Whatever his son did or didn't know about his activities was irrelevant. It was what he might know about the rest of his family that interested me.

"How often did your father meet with his brother, Muhammad Ibrahim?" I asked. With Farris Yasin and Radman effectively out of the picture, my attention had naturally turned to the other important member of the Al-Muslit bodyguard fraternity. Over the course of dozens of interrogations and source meetings I had heard the name Muhammad Ibrahim come up on a constant basis. He was the only remaining brother with the power and influence to hold the operation together.

"Muhammad never came to our house."

"Don't lie to me!" I shouted. "I know your father saw his brother many times. How many times?"

"My father used to go to Baghdad," Baby Radman answered with a whimper. "Perhaps they met there."

"Perhaps?" I repeated the word contemptuously. "We're not playing a guessing game here, asshole."

"Muhammad Ibrahim has friends. Ask them."

This was interesting. "What friends?" I asked. "What are their names?"

Baby Radman seemed relived to be off the subject of his father. "His driver," he told me. "Basim Latif."

I didn't recognize the name. "That's his driver," I said. "We're talking about his friends."

"A business partner. Abu Drees."

"Drivers. Business partners. What about his friends? That's

what I want to know." I was actually getting what I wanted, but it was important to keep the kid off guard.

"Those are his friends," he insisted. "They are always together."

I had a problem here. I knew that as soon as Baby Radman was released he would report to his family everything he'd been asked. It was critical that he not know exactly which particular individuals I was interested in. I had never heard of Basim Latif or Abu Drees before. But they were coming up fast on my most wanted list. I just needed to make sure Baby Radman didn't realize that.

I spent the next two hours grilling him on other Al-Muslit family members and their respective best friends. It was only after the extensive detour that I brought the questioning back around.

"This driver of Muhammad Ibrahim. What's his name again?"

"Basim Latif."

"Yeah, that's the guy. And where does he live?"

"His house is behind the governor's mansion."

"And the business partner?"

"Abu Drees. He has a store that sells rock and stones for construction. It is owned by Muhammad Ibrahim."

That was the information I was after. If I could just convince Kelly and Bam Bam, then these locations would be the next targets for a hit. But to cover my tracks, I spent another hour going over more details of friends and family before finally letting Baby Radman go.

"We need to put a couple more guys on the link diagram," I told Kelly when I returned to the house.

"I'm sure you have your reasons," he said, after I told him

about Basim Latif and Abu Drees. "But we can't just go after someone because they used to know Muhammad Ibrahim."

"I need to find these guys, Kelly," I replied.

"Look," he said with an edge to his voice. "You keep going down on this fucking link diagram and we'll never get anywhere. We're supposed to be working our way up. But you're just adding names to the bottom of the list."

"I know," I said, "But if I can't go up then I've got to go down. And if I can't go down than I can't go anywhere—"

"Eric," he interrupted. "We have to justify bringing in low-level people that haven't done anything. Muhammad Ibrahim may be at the top of your list, but he doesn't mean shit in Baghdad. Now you want his driver and his business partner. How are we going to explain that?"

I could tell he was frustrated. So was I. If I couldn't sell this to Kelly, I couldn't sell it to anyone. And for the moment, he wasn't buying.

$$\star \; \star \; \star$$

Despite Kelly's skepticism, I knew I had to find a way to make this happen. With Radman dead and Farris Yasin still tight-lipped, the driver and the business partner provided the only link I had left to Muhammad Ibrahim. I desperately needed to bring in Basim Latif and Abu Drees.

Fortunately help arrived from a very unlikely source. The morning after my session with Baby Radman, I was scheduled for a source meeting with Fred. Chris's old informant had been keeping track of the street gangs in Tikrit that were aiding the insurgency. My intention was only to find out if he'd learned anything new about Munthir, the thug who ran the largest and most vicious of these groups. But once I sat him down I had another idea. It wouldn't hurt to ask him what he knew about Muhammad Ibrahim.

"He is very important, mister," Fred told me.

That much I already knew. "Do you ever see Muhammad Ibrahim?"

"Before the war, but not now," he explained.

"You ever heard of someone named Abu Drees?" I continued.

He grinned. "He is a friend of Muhammad Ibrahim. I know where he is. I can take you to his house. He lives next door to Ahmad Hussein."

"And who is Ahmad Hussein?"

"A very bad man," Fred assured me. "He has RPGs. He has shot down two American helicopters."

A man in Tikrit with a rocket-propelled grenade launcher and a grudge against Americans was hardly news. I'd had dozens of such reports from detainees since I'd arrived, most of them bullshit. I was about to add Fred's to the pile. He wasn't the most reliable source I'd ever worked with. But then I got an idea.

"Fred, can you call me when Abu Drees and Ahmad Hussein are both at home?"

"Mister, I give you good information all the time. You never do anything with it."

"Just call me," I repeated and hurried off to find Kelly.

I found him back at the house and ran down the information I'd just gotten. "I think these are good hits," I added.

"Where did you get this?" Kelly asked skeptically.

"Fred," I said under my breath.

He laughed out loud. He knew Fred's reputation only too well.

"Look, Kelly," I said, talking fast, "I know what you're thinking. This chopper thing may not be real. But Abu Drees is. And he's going to tell us where Muhammad Ibrahim is. All we need is a reason to do the hit. Now we've got one."

"Did this guy Ahmed Hussein really shoot down a helicopter?" Kelly asked dubiously.

"Maybe," I said without conviction. "Somebody had to have shot them down. Maybe it's this guy. Will you push for the hits?"

He gave me a long silent stare. I took it as a yes.

Six hours later we had completed a successful raid on the two objectives. I was in the guesthouse with Abu Drees, wondering if I'd made a mistake. He was an old man, confused and disoriented. I tried patiently to build his timeline, but the dates kept contradicting one another and the facts didn't add up. Words were coming out of his mouth but nothing was connecting. I wondered if he was maybe senile or if it was just an act. I needed another way to get at this guy.

I found it when I began interrogating his son Akail, who had also been rounded up in the raid and was being kept in a separate room, along with Abu Drees's younger son, Ahmed, who had also been captured. Akail was a huge guy, over six feet and easily two hundred and fifty pounds. But he was also clearly terrified. It was a condition that once again could prove very useful to my purposes.

He answered the preliminary questions as if, more than anything, he wanted me to tell him how to stay out of trouble. I did nothing to reassure him, patiently piling facts until the time was right to make my move. "Your dad says he is in business with Muhammad Ibrahim," I said. Abu Drees had said nothing of the sort, but I needed a way to get the ball rolling.

"I don't know who that is," he replied evasively.

"Come on, Akail. Everyone knows Muhammad Ibrahim. He's your dad's best friend."

He swallowed hard. It was obvious that his fear was at odds with his family loyalty. "They own a few buildings together," he said at last. "That is all I know."

I returned to Abu Drees. From here on out, my strategy was simple: play the father off the son and the other way around.

"Your son tells me you are very close to Muhammad Ibrahim," I said. "He says you own property together."

"Yes," Abu Drees replied, squinting at me as if trying to figure out what I knew and what I was pretending to know. "Sometimes we drink and play cards together."

"Your son tells me you still see him very often."

Abu Drees shook his head. "Not since the war began," he lied.

"That's not what Akail says."

"My son knows nothing," he insisted.

"I'll tell him you said so," I replied as I went out the door and down the hall to where Akail was waiting.

"All you know is that your dad and Muhammad Ibrahim own some buildings?" I asked the frightened hulk. "What about the drinking and the card games. Did you forget about that, you piece of shit?" I dropped my voice to a hoarse whisper. I was after maximum effect. "Your dad can't tell me about Muhammad Ibrahim, Akail. He wants to, but he can't because he is afraid. This is your fault. You can help him but you won't." I opened the door and called to the guard. A moment later he escorted in the shuffling and miserable Abu Drees. He was drenched with sweat and his hands, cuffed behind him, trembled violently. "Look at your dad!" I shouted at Akail. "He may die in prison and you won't help him." It was generally against protocol to interrogate more than one prisoner at the same time. But I had no choice. One of these two had to talk to me. There was no other way that was going to happen.

"Take him away, please!" sobbed Akail. "Help him! I will tell you what you want to know."

One of the operators hustled Abu Drees out and I waited a few minutes while Akail pulled himself together. "Muhammad Ibrahim was with my father two weeks ago," he said at last, his voice barely above a whisper. "I swear to you."

"Where?"

"They played dominoes at a store. It is owned by a man named Thamir Al-Asi. He has two sons. They help him."

"Who else was there?"

"Basim Latif. He is the driver for Muhammad Ibrahim. They are always together."

"You're going to take me there."

"Muhammad Ibrahim is gone," he wailed. "I have told you everything I know."

"Don't ever say that again!" I shouted, getting into his face. "You don't know what I want to know. You don't even know what you don't know. I'll tell you when you're done."

But, in fact, we were both done. It was 0600 the next day. I had been interrogating Abu Drees and his two sons, Akail and Ahmed, virtually nonstop for thirty straight hours. Leaving Akail to think over his options, I made my way back to the house and crawled into bed. It wasn't until my head hit the pillow that I realized that I forgotten to question the helicopter guy. By then it was too late. I was sound asleep.

CHAPTER 11

THE DRIVER

2000 16NOV2003

It turned out that the guy who was supposed to be shooting down our choppers with RPGs was completely innocent. His only crime was being our source's landlord. Fred just didn't want to pay his rent and figured that the Americans could solve his problem for him. I had to hand it to Fred. He really knew how to work the angles. And despite the fact that the hit he sent us on had been total bullshit, it had gotten me Abu Drees. And that had gotten me one step closer to Muhammad Ibrahim.

By now I was convinced that the Al-Muslits had graduated from being Saddam's elite bodyguards to being the leadership core of the insurgency. I may not have been able to prove my theory absolutely, but nothing had disproved it either. In fact, I continued to get good intelligence that told me I was on the right track.

Several key pieces of information had come together to point me in the direction of Thamir Al-Asi. He was the same friend of Muhammad Ibrahim whose name I first heard from the son of Abu Drees. Thamir and his own two sons, Amir and

Ahmed, ran a small cement store in Tikrit. Muhammad Ibrahim had occasionally dropped by to play dominoes. From my interrogations of Abu Drees and his sons, I discovered that Thamir was more than just a friend. He actually served as the proprietor for properties that he owned jointly with Muhammad Ibrahim, including the cement store. Several nearby residences were also part of Thamir Al-Asi and Muhammad Ibrahim's extensive real estate holdings. More interesting still was the fact that he apparently owned the house where his former driver Basim Latif lived. The network of Al-Muslit associates and beneficiaries was now coming clear. Muhammad Ibrahim had three cronies, Abu Drees, Basim Latif, and Thamir Al-Asi. I had learned of their existence from my interrogation of Baby Radman and they had since made a quick move up our link diagram.

More valuable intelligence surfaced in mid-November when Shakir, who along with Abu Qasar was one of Farris Yasin's closest associates, turned himself in to the local police. I immediately interrogated him and he proved to be a very informative subject. At first he refused to admit any connection to Farris Yasin or to have any knowledge of his activities. But after several intense hours I was finally able to break him down. He then went on to detail for me the authority structure that held the Al-Muslit operation together.

"I was working for Farris, and Farris was working for Radman," he explained. "I never saw Radman. Only Farris, I swear."

"And who does Radman work for?"

He shrugged. "I don't know. But I heard it was for his brother, Muhammad Ibrahim."

"When was the last time you saw Muhammad Ibrahim?"

"It has been many months. Since before the war."

"Are you a friend of his?"

He laughed, as if the idea was absurd. "I was friends with Farris," he replied. "I knew Radman a little. But Muhammad Ibrahim is different."

"How different?"

"Mister, aside from Abid Mahmood, his personal secretary, there was no one Saddam trusted more that Muhammad Ibrahim."

It was exactly what I wanted to hear. Everything we'd done since I'd arrived in Tikrit—focusing on the bodyguards, tracking down the Al-Muslits, constructing a link diagram one suspect at a time—all came down to a single goal: finding Saddam. Shakir's information was another vital part of the puzzle.

The problem was, I was running out of time. My tour of duty was coming to an end and I was scheduled to return to the States no later than December 15. With the out-processing factored in, that meant I had about three weeks left in Tikrit to get the job done.

To me the next step was obvious. I had to talk to Basim Latif, who had been identified by both Baby Radman and the son of Abu Drees as Muhammad Ibrahim's driver and close friend. I wanted to get him as soon as possible. But that was easier said than done.

"We already hit the helicopter guy," Kelly protested when I brought up the subject of bringing in Basim. "We're probably not going to get approved for another nobody."

"Basim isn't a nobody, Kelly," I replied. "He could take us to Muhammad Ibrahim. And Muhammad Ibrahim could lead us to . . ." I paused. The last thing I wanted was to create expectations I couldn't fulfill.

"Look, Eric," Kelly said with an exasperated sigh. "I told

you. We have to move *up* the ladder. Basim Latif, Abu Drees and whoever else hung out with Muhammad Ibrahim are all sideways targets. If we're going after Muhammad Ibrahim, let's focus on him. He's our next move."

Now it was my turn to be exasperated. "If Muhammad Ibrahim is our next move, then we don't have a next move. I don't know where he is and I don't know how to find him. Basim can tell us. He knows where to find him. We have to bring him in."

It was a hard sell. Nobody else grasped the potential importance of Basim. I had already found that out through my connections with the 4th ID's tactical HUMINT teams and the 4th ID military police battalion. Part of their job was to keep tabs on the actions of low-level thugs and insurgents throughout Tikrit. They had compiled long lists of names, often followed by a one- or two-word description of the suspected activity: IED maker, financier, etc. I had been looking through these pages one afternoon when I came across Basim Latif's name. "Cousin of Chief" was the notation that followed it. Basim, it turned out, was the nephew of the powerful chief of security for the governor of Tikrit.

"What do you know about this Basim Latif?" I asked the MP lieutenant.

He shrugged. "I'm not sure," he said. "He was arrested by the local police. His uncle arranged to get him out of prison if he would become a source for us."

"Are you getting information from him?"

"We haven't talked to him yet. The battalion commander has been working to maintain a good relationship with the chief. This may have just been a way for us to do him a favor."

"Listen," I replied. "You'd be doing me a favor if you can arrange for Basim to come in so I can talk to him."

Three weeks after his arrest, Basim Latif was suddenly on our side. And that was going to make it even harder to get what I needed out of him. As a source working for us, Basim would have no incentive to reveal what he knew. For that to happen he would have to be a prisoner with the threat of open-ended incarceration hanging over his head. That was my primary reason for wanting him to be in my custody. But it was a sensitive situation. There was no way I could just arrest a close family member of the governor's security chief. As the lieutenant had told me, the brass at the 4th ID had spent a lot of time building an alliance with the governor of Tikrit. They were not about to allow that relationship to be compromised.

I could understand why. The governor of Tikrit was just about the only Sunni friend we had in the whole Sunni Triangle. Pissing him off could conceivably lead to complaints passed up the line to the highest military and political levels. My only option was to talk with Basim on his terms and hope I could work around his built-in immunity. Since the head of the 4th ID's military police had a special relationship with the Tikrit officials, my meeting with Basim would have to be arranged by them. The commanding officer agreed on the condition that the interview took place at the military police headquarters and under no circumstance would we be allowed to arrest the driver.

Basim might have been about forty-five, but the desert sun had aged him at least ten years. Several more years, and a few pounds, had been added by hard drinking. He seemed happy to help and anxious to please, knowing that he needed to appear to be in full compliance with the arrangement his uncle had worked out. But he wasn't about to give up any useful information about his former employer.

"Why were you arrested, Basim?" I asked, trying my best to come off as friendly.

"I used to be Muhammad Ibrahim's driver," he replied. "You are looking for Muhammad Ibrahim. The police thought I could be of help."

"Can you?"

He shrugged, smiling serenely.

"How long were you his driver?"

"For two years."

"Did you see him every day?"

"Not every day."

"Did you drive for him after the war?"

"Yes, I was still his driver."

"Are you still his driver now?"

"I have not seen him for a month."

"But you're still his driver."

Basim spoke slowly, as if he was explaining the facts to a child. "I was arrested," he said. "Then I was released. He no longer trusts me. He thinks I am a spy for the Americans."

"Are you a spy?"

"Yes. I swore to my cousin that I would do everything I could to help you."

"So help us."

He smirked. "How can I help?"

"Where did you last see Muhammad Ibrahim?"

"I was walking down the street. I saw him drive by in a car."

"Why weren't you driving him?"

He sighed. "I told you, mister. He no longer trusts me."

"Where is Muhammad Ibrahim now?"

"I don't know. I will try to help you find him."

"How will you do that?"

"I will lay low for a while until he starts to trust me again. Then they will come to me."

"Who is 'they'?"

"Muhammad Ibrahim has many people."

"Who are the ones closest to him?"

"Abu Drees."

"Anyone else?"

Basim shrugged again. The fact that he had named Abu Drees wasn't surprising. He must have known that we had arrested him and there was no downside to implicating the old man. What was revealing was the fact that Basim hadn't mentioned Thamir Al-Asi or his two sons. If he was really committed to cooperating with us, he would have offered up anyone and everyone he could think of who was a friend or associate of his former boss.

"Will these people help you find Muhammad Ibrahim?"

He nodded. "They will take me to him. Then he will look me in the eye and decide if he trusts me."

Basim was not the first to tell me that an Iraqi could stare eyeball-to-eyeball and decide whether someone was loyal. I didn't have that ability, but I didn't need it to know that Basim had no intention of helping us find Muhammad Ibrahim. As long as he had the protection of the cousin, the chief of security, there was no incentive for him to cooperate. Maybe he was still involved with his old boss or maybe not. All he had to do now was lie low and see which side, the Americans or the insurgency, best served his interests.

As soon as I was finished questioning Basim Latif, I took Kelly aside. "We need to arrest that guy," I told him with absolute conviction. "He's lying through his teeth. I need an honest

Basim and I'm not going to get that until he's scared. Really scared."

"You are going to have to sell it to Bam Bam," Kelly said and together we went looking for him.

We found him in the dining room. Sitting down at the table, the three of us discussed the available options. I ran down what I had heard from Basim, what he claimed to know, and what I thought he was concealing from us. I wanted to make sure that Bam Bam understood the connection between Abu Drees, Basim Latif, and Thamir Al-Asi. They were the three men closest to Muhammad Ibrahim. They all knew each other and, between them, I was sure that we would be able to track down our primary target.

Basim was the next logical step, but we all knew that by arresting the driver, Bam Bam would be taking a huge risk. It was ultimately his ass on the line and he'd have to take the heat for any political shit that hit the fan as a result. But at the same time, both he and Kelly knew that I might be onto something big. The fact that we never mentioned Saddam by name didn't mean we weren't all thinking of the possibility of his capture. It was that unspoken but very real potential that was being weighed in the balance.

"What do you want me to do, Eric?" Bam Bam asked, cutting to the chase.

I thought for a moment. "I want you to listen to Basim when I question him," I said, slowly and deliberately. "I've told you what I think he knows. If you don't agree that he's lying or holding back information, then I'll stop asking you to arrest him. But if you think I'm right, then we need to take him into custody and treat him like any other prisoner."

"What's he going to lie about?" Kelly asked.

"I don't know," I replied. "But I'll get him to do it and when he does, you'll know he's holding back. I guarantee it."

"Listen, Eric," Bam Bam said, and his tone of voice got my full attention. "This is going to draw more attention to us than we ever wanted. And it can blow up in our faces. We're supposed to be leaving this country someday and when that happens we're going to turn it over to our allies. Right now, one of those allies is the governor of Tikrit. He's more important in Washington and Baghdad than you or I will ever be."

We sat in silence for what seemed like a long time. "So what do you want to do, Bam Bam?" Kelly finally asked.

He looked at me and I could see in his eyes the weight of the decision he had to make. "Let's go talk to this son-of-a-bitch, Basim," he said.

★ ★ ★

It would be a few days before the 4th ID could arrange the meeting. I spent Thanksgiving with Bam Bam, Kelly, and the terps. The rest of the shooters had been called to Baghdad to serve as a personal security detachment for President Bush, who had come to Iraq for a holiday morale boost.

It might seem like that Thanksgiving was a lonely interlude in a hostile country a long way from home. But instead it was an opportunity for me to reflect on everything I had experienced over the last several months. In that period of time I had become completely engrossed in my work. I realized I had no real idea what was going on in the rest of Iraq or, for that matter, back in the States. About the only connection I maintained to my former life was the Sooners. I needed them to win more than ever. There was a relief in watching those games in the late hours of a Saturday night, seeing all those joyful, innocent fans fill a stadium and basking in the pride of the Sooners. The fact that they were dismantling the competition was an added bonus. For a few hours I was able to escape from the tensions and anger and deception that I dealt with every day.

I called my wife and children as often as I could. But there was something about hearing their voices so far away that made me understand that I wasn't really doing all this for them. I needed this war and I needed to be a part of it for my own selfish reasons. The bottom line was that I'd signed up to be a warrior. Soldiers are happiest when they are fighting. Rebuilding a country was a noble goal, but the real reason we were there was to destroy the enemy.

That Thanksgiving night, I found myself thinking about my friend Casey again. I pictured him sitting at that bar in heaven with the other heroes in my life. They were warriors, too, and I was still trying to earn my place next to them.

☆ ☆ ☆

It was on December 1, with the clock still ticking on my tour of duty, that I finally got word I would have another chance to question Basim Latif. Not only would Bam Bam and Kelly be present, but the entire team was going to show up for the session. It was scheduled to be held at the offices of the mayor of Tikrit, housed in a large three-story office building.

While the shooters had occasionally dropped by the guesthouse to watch my interrogations in the past, this was something different. It was as if, without a word being said, they all understood how much was riding on my confrontation with Basim. They wanted to be there when it went down. Despite the fact that I would now have an audience, I felt strangely calm. We were in this together, from Bam Bam to the most junior operator. Any success that might come from what was about to happen would be a success we would all share.

The streets of Tikrit were empty as we rode to the mayor's mansion. It was a quick trip out of the wire and I had one last opportunity to think about what I needed to do: convince Bam Bam to arrest a well-connected and seemingly innocent citizen of Tikrit.

I reviewed the facts in my head. Basim Latif was the former driver of Muhammad Ibrahim, the next link in the long chain of Al-Muslit bodyguards I'd assembled on the link diagram. I was pretty sure Basim could take us to his old boss if I could get him to open up. Then Muhammad Ibrahim, a trusted adviser of Saddam, might be able to take us to *his* old boss.

But Basim was also the cousin of one of Tikrit's top-ranking security chiefs. His responsibility was to guard the Sunni governor of the city. By supporting the Americans, the governor had made himself a prime insurgent target. The fact that he was even still alive was proof that his security chief was a powerful man. If he didn't want his cousin arrested, he could make real trouble for us.

What we were about to do was risky in all kinds of ways. I ran down the worst-case scenario in my mind as we made our way through town. If Bam Bam actually authorized the arrest of Basim, he'd be putting his career on the line. But I also knew that bringing in Basim was our best shot at getting one step closer to Saddam. Without Basim, I'd come to a dead end.

I wiped my forehead with the sleeve of my blue oxford shirt, the one I'd been wearing on and off between T-shirts for over four months now. We had reached the barbed wire perimeter of the mayor's office, patrolled by local police and Iraqi military, as well as U.S. troops. They immediately escorted us through a maze of hallways to the security chief's office. As we arrived at the heavy wooden door, I glanced over at Bam Bam. I knew he still hadn't made up his mind whether or not to arrest Basim. He would weigh his options as they unfolded.

The chief was a supremely self-confident officer, well groomed with a crisp, clean uniform. He was polite, even soft-spoken. Regardless of what was at stake, this was all going to be very courteous and respectful.

"My cousin is not here at the moment," he said as we entered. "My men will bring him." Then he started with his version of the speech I'd heard delivered so many times before by Iraqis to Americans. "I want you to know how pleased I am that we have been able to support you and your mission to make Iraq a safe and free country. We are working as brothers to complete this mission. I am sure my cousin Basim will be a very valuable asset to you."

Bam Bam didn't miss a beat. "Chief, if Basim is being completely honest, there will be no problem."

"I can assure you my cousin will be honest with you," the chief replied. "I give you my word. In turn, I would like your assurance that you will not take Basim with you."

"If he's telling the truth, that won't be a problem," Bam Bam repeated.

"As I said, you have my word." The chief was clearly prepared to stand up for his cousin. This could get ugly.

The door opened again and Basim was escorted in. He seemed in good spirits and exchanged the traditional kisses on the cheek with his older cousin. Then he turned to us with a sly smile. Bam Bam caught my eye and gave me an unmistakable cue: it was showtime.

The room was crowded with spectators, including six operators from our team and some 4th Infantry Division MPs, backed up against the wall to watch the performance. I figured I had about forty-five minutes to prove Basim was lying about something, anything. And it probably wouldn't be nearly that long before the chief stepped in if he thought I was trying to humiliate his cousin.

Basim and I sat down at a small table and I started by asking a few simple questions: How was his health? Was he married? How many children did he have? His answers were quick and confident. But he was also guarded. He kept glancing at the cousin, as if to make sure he still had his support.

"How much money did you make driving for Muhammad Ibrahim?" I asked, suddenly changing direction after running through the routine information gathering.

"Four hundred American dollars," he replied. "But I have not been paid in months. My rent alone is one hundred and fifty dollars and I am three months behind." I made a mental note of his response. It wasn't information I'd asked for, but it might come in handy.

The questions and answers continued at a rapid clip. Basim repeated much of the story he had told me previously, emphasizing that since his arrest he was no longer trusted by Muhammad Ibrahim.

I leaned forward. "Basim, we let you go the first time because you said you could help us find Muhammad Ibrahim. Now you're telling us that he doesn't trust you. If you can't help us anymore, why shouldn't we just arrest you again?"

"Because Muhammad Ibrahim is still in Tikrit," he replied. "I can help you find him."

"How do you know he's in Tikrit?"

"I saw him, with my own eyes, just two days ago."

This was something new. When I'd questioned Basim eight days earlier, he'd claimed to have not seen his old boss for a month. "Where was he?" I asked

"At the market in the New Oja district. But I don't know where he went after that."

"Did he live in New Oja?"

Basim nodded. "Before the war. He had a house there."

"That's where you used to pick him up?"

"Sometimes."

"How far was it from your house to his house?"

He considered. "Perhaps eight kilometers," he guessed.

"So you saw Muhammad Ibrahim in the New Oja market two days ago?"

"Yes, mister."

"Why didn't you report it to us?"

"I have no phone," he replied. "If you will provide a phone I will call you the next time I see him."

"Why were you late today?" I asked, trying another angle. "You say you want to help, but you don't even arrive in time for an important meeting."

"Because I have no car anymore," he replied. "My brother is trying to sell it for me in Syria."

"You were in the New Oja market two days ago," I reminded him. "How did you get there?"

Basim looked uncomfortable. "I . . . walked," he stammered.

I gave a low whistle. "That's clear across town. It must be sixteen kilometers there and back."

He nodded nervously.

"So you're telling me you walked sixteen kilometers to New

Oja where you just happened to see Muhammad Ibrahim, but you couldn't walk the five hundred meters from your house to here?"

He just stared at me. I needed to keep him off-balance now. "How much money are you going to make from selling your car?"

"Twelve hundred dollars."

"What are you going to do with it?"

"Pay my rent," he replied cautiously.

The rent again. I suddenly realized why it had caught my attention the first time he brought it up. I ripped a piece of paper from my notepad, jotted down a note, and put it in my shirt pocket. I made sure that everyone in the room saw what I was doing, specifically Bam Bam.

"Where do you go to pay your rent?" I asked Basim.

"A small store," he answered. I could see him wondering where this was going. "Down at the intersection."

"What do they sell at this store?"

"I think it is cement."

"You think?"

He looked wary. "It is cement."

"Who runs the store?"

"I do not know, mister." I could see the fear on his face now, and hear the tremor in his voice.

"Come on, Basim, you've lived in Tikrit your whole life. You know everyone and their uncle. Who runs the store?"

A long silence followed. "I think," he replied in a hoarse whisper, "it is a man named Amir."

"Amir *what*?" I shouted.

"Amir Al-Asi," he replied, staring at the table.

I took out the piece of notepaper and without unfolding it,

handed it to Bam Bam. He opened it and glanced back at me with a nod.

"Thamir Al-Asi is an associate of Muhammad Ibrahim and a close friend to Basim Latif," he read silently. "He runs a cement store with his two sons, Amir and Ahmed."

My intent had been to let Bam Bam know that I had anticipated where this would be going. In fact, I really hadn't been sure until the driver started talking about paying his rent. At that point, I put together his story with the accounts I'd been given about Muhammad Ibrahim actually owning the cement store and the house where Basim and his family lived. His landlord was Muhammad Ibrahim, and there was no way Basim could not have known that.

If Basim had admitted up front that he was living, most likely rent free, in a house provided by his former boss, he would have proven where his loyalty lay. But instead he was trying to hide his close connection to the man we were after. Basim had tipped his hand. It was there for everyone, but most importantly Bam Bam, to see.

"Basim," I continued. "Who really owns your house?"

"I do not know," he stammered. "I know only Amir. I am trying to help you, mister." It was apparent that he didn't want to bring up the name of Thamir Al-Asi and was trying to throw us off the track by only mentioning his son Amir.

The chief stepped forward. "It is time for me to pray," he said abruptly. He obviously didn't like the direction the interrogation was taking. In less than an hour, I had established that his cousin was lying about his willingness to work on our side. More important, Basim still had direct ties to Muhammad Ibrahim that he was hiding from everyone, including his uncle.

Bam Bam ordered the 4th Infantry MPs to take Basim into

another room. He gestured for me to follow him into the hall. "So what now?" he asked when we were alone.

"Bam Bam," I said, "I need this guy. And I need him in custody. He's the key to Muhammad Ibrahim, and Muhammad Ibrahim is the key to Saddam." It was the first time I'd actually spoken the connection out loud. There was no turning back now. It was all on Bam Bam.

"Eric," he said, "if we bring this guy in today, you're going to have to produce some results fast. Either that or you're going to come to CENTCOM with me to explain to General Abizaid how we got the entire U.S. military on the mayor of Tikrit's shit list."

I took that as a yes, we were going to arrest Basim.

We returned to the chief's office where Bam Bam cut directly to the chase. "Your cousin is not being honest, sir," he said. "I'm sorry, but he has to come with us."

"I will take full responsibility for Basim," was the chief's rattled reply. "He will be your best source, I guarantee. He will live inside my house and you will have access to him whenever you wish."

Bam Bam just shook his head. "He lied to you and he lied to us."

I could see the jaws of the 4th Infantry guys collectively drop. They hadn't believed for a minute that we would actually take Basim with us. And I could almost see them gleefully anticipating what kind of trouble we were getting ourselves into. But Bam Bam never blinked, and neither did the other shooters. In that moment, I was never more proud to be a part of their team.

But even as we walked back out to the Humvees, I knew that the hard work was just beginning. And Bam Bam confirmed it when he turned to me and said, "Eric, I need whatever targets you get from Basim, asap."

CHAPTER 12

THE SPIGOT

1430 01DEC2003

As soon as I got Basim back to the guesthouse, I came down on him fast and furious. I had wanted to start off slower and try to build a rapport. But since he had stuck to his story about only wanting to be a fully cooperative source, he left me no option.

It took me an hour just to convince him that he was no longer considered a friend. From here on out, he was a prisoner and would be treated accordingly. The reasons were simple: he had a past association with a suspected leader of the insurgency, he had provided inaccurate or false answers when questioned by U.S. personnel, and he could potentially put coalition forces in harm's way if he was released.

His response was to insist that if we held him, he would lose any possibility of regaining Muhammad Ibrahim's trust. The harder I pushed, the more he dug in his heels. He down-played his association with his old boss, claiming he was little more than a glorified taxi driver. I think he wanted me to get a picture of him driving Muhammad Ibrahim from behind a glass window, shut off from any contact with his passenger. He had no idea what was going on in the backseat of his own car. If that were true, I pointed out, then Muhammad Ibrahim would have no reason to be concerned that Basim had been arrested. If there was nothing he could tell us that would implicate Muhammad Ibrahim, why would he need to regain his trust?

He didn't have a good answer for that, so I moved on. My next area of interest was Thamir Al-Asi, the cement store proprietor and Muhammad Ibrahim's alleged business partner. While I knew that Thamir should be our next hit regardless of what Basim revealed, I didn't let him know that. Instead I suggested that if Basim would tell us where our target was, we would have no reason to roll up Thamir. If he didn't, we'd have to move on to the next potential source of intelligence that would lead to Muhammad Ibrahim.

"There is no need to arrest Thamir," Basim insisted. "He will not know where Muhammad Ibrahim is."

"Did you ever drive him to Thamir's house?" I asked.

"Many times."

"Did he ever stay the night there?"

"Yes."

"So why wouldn't he be there now?"

"Since I have been arrested," he replied, "Muhammad Ibrahim has been in hiding. He thinks I am working for you and that I will tell you everything he does. So now, he will change everything. He will not go back to Thamir Al-Asi's house again."

He was giving me another opening and I took it. "He's going to change everything because you know everything, Basim," I shot back. "He's worried because we've arrested you. He knows what you could tell us if you wanted to. But you don't want to, do you, Basim? You're playing a game with us. You're wasting my time. I'm going to pick up Thamir because you've left me no choice. And you're going to come with me. That way, everyone will know that you're working for us. I'll make sure of that." I leaned in close. "And I'll also make sure that you'll spend the rest of your life in prison."

Basim's eyes bounced from my face to the wall and back again. It was finally getting through. He was beginning to understand that his choices had just narrowed drastically.

"You won't find Muhammad Ibrahim," he finally said. "He is not in Tikrit anymore."

"Basim, you told me you saw him in the market a few days ago."

"It is not true. I did not see him."

"So," I said, still inches from his face, "if he's not in Tikrit, then where is he?"

"I heard he was in Samarra."

"Why Samarra?"

"So many of his relatives have been arrested here," Basim explained. "He was fearful they would turn on him."

"What is Muhammad Ibrahim's role in the insurgency?"

There was another long silence. Then Basim began to smile. "You really don't know?" he asked contemptuously.

"I'm asking the questions here, asshole," I shouted. "Who does Muhammad Ibrahim report to?"

"Who do you think?" he sneered.

"Don't fuck with me, Basim. Answer the question."

"He reports to the president," he said, knowing full well the impact that his statement would have.

I felt my gut lurch. For the first time, I had established a direct link between Muhammad Ibrahim and Saddam. I took a step back and gave Basim a long hard stare. He glared back, as if daring me to call him a liar. The fact was, I believed him.

However else the driver was trying to deceive me, there was no reason for him to connect his old boss to Saddam Hussein. We had turned a corner and we both knew it.

"So Muhammad Ibrahim reports to the president," I repeated as calmly as I could. "Who reports to Muhammad Ibrahim?"

"They all do." Basim answered as if he could hardly be bothered with such an obvious question.

"Who is 'they'?" I pressed.

"Everyone," he replied. "They all work for him."

"Who does he give orders to? Who sees him face-to-face?"

"Only a few," Basim replied. "Mostly his brother Radman. He was in charge of Baghdad and Tikrit and places in the west."

"Radman is dead, Basim. Give me someone who is still breathing."

I took a deep breath. The information was coming rapidly now. It was as if I had turned on a spigot in Basim's brain. Once I'd tapped it, the names and places came pouring out and in the next few minutes Basim revealed the primary insurgency leaders in both Fallujah and Samarra. "They are in charge," he said and I detected a note of pride in his voice, as if he was pleased to know these important men.

"What do you mean in charge?" I asked. "What are they in charge of?"

"All the attacks," he replied. "They take their orders from Muhammad Ibrahim. Then he pays them."

"How much?"

Basim's tone was still arrogant. "I always had a few hundred thousand dollars in my trunk," he said. "Muhammad Ibrahim would give it out as he needed to."

I looked at the terp. "Did you get that number right?" I asked.

Jimmy nodded. "Hundreds of thousands of dollars," he repeated. "He's talking about U.S. dollars, sir."

As with bringing up Saddam, Basim was sending me a signal by talking about such huge sums of money. This was serious business being done by serious people with a serious purpose. I was way past the point of interrogating low-level detainees who'd been caught in the wrong place at the wrong time. This wasn't about informants interested only in turning a quick profit. Despite the enormous risk it posed, arresting Basim was the breakthrough I'd been waiting for. I was on the inside now, getting a firsthand look at the insurgency and the men who had ordered the deaths of thousands of Americans and Iraqis.

"Where is Muhammad Ibrahim now?" I asked Basim directly. If he was telling the truth about everything else, maybe he'd give me the answer to the single most important question I had.

"I don't know," he replied. "But perhaps I can help you find him."

"Basim," I said, heaving an exaggerated sigh. "You're not going anywhere until Muhammad Ibrahim is sitting where you're sitting. As soon as you understand that, we can make some progress."

He looked at me and I could see all the arrogance draining away. The situation had finally sunk in. "I understand," he said softly.

"Good. Now, where does Muhammad Ibrahim sleep?"

"He was staying at his family farm on the other side of the river after the war."

"Is he still there?"

He shook his head. "It was raided by the Americans. One of his cousins was captured. He never went back. Since this summer he was always with Thamir Al-Asi and Abu Drees."

"He slept at the house of Abu Drees?"

"I cannot say for sure. He would have me drop him off in the New Oja neighborhood at night and he would tell me to pick him up the next morning at a market or a tea shop or the cement store that he owned with Thamir Al-Asi. They would play dominoes there."

"Basim," I said, locking onto his eyes. "Where do I go to find him now?"

"There is a man," he replied. "They were working together. His name is Abu Sofian."

"Who is Abu Sofian?"

"In Samarra he is responsible for every attack and bombing." I could hear the admiration in his voice. I was impressed myself. Over the past several months, American soldiers were constantly getting lit up in Samarra. It was one of the most dangerous places in the entire country.

"So where does this Abu Sofian live?"

He shook his head. "He is dead, mister. He died a few weeks ago."

"I told you Basim. I don't need dead people."

"Mister, Muhammad Ibrahim thought I was the reason Abu Sofian was killed. He never trusted me after that."

"So how are you going to gain his trust back, Basim?"

"Mister, I just didn't want you to arrest me. I have not seen Muhammad Ibrahim since Abu Sofian was killed."

"Did you get him killed?"

"No. But Muhammad Ibrahim was so angry he needed to blame someone."

I sat down in front of him, almost knee to knee. "Let's take this from the top. How many children does Muhammad Ibrahim have?"

"He had a son who is eighteen years old. There are three younger children. And his wife had a baby three months ago."

This was useful information. Muhammad Ibrahim had family obligations. With so many mouths to feed, he would have to maintain contact in some way to make sure his children were being cared for. "Where does his wife live?" I asked.

"At her father's house, here in Tikrit. She sent the children to live with relatives."

"Where in Tikrit does she live?"

He laughed. "In Old Oja," he replied. "The Americans have barricaded the neighborhood. He feels safe with her there."

"Does Muhammad Ibrahim come to see her?"

"Mister, I told you. Your soldiers guard it. There is no way he can come. But perhaps they meet somewhere else. Maybe you will find him at his farm. Or . . ." he paused.

"Or what?"

"There is a prostitute that Muhammad Ibrahim sometimes visits," he told me. I could see his reluctance to admit his old boss's preference for hookers. "Perhaps he is staying there."

"All right," I said. "Who else do I need to know about?"

He thought for a moment. He was either trying to remember other names or trying to find a way to avoid revealing them to me. But that option had already been closed out. He knew it and I knew it. He had already given me more than enough information to get him killed by the insurgents. There was no reason to stop now. We were the only ones that could keep him alive.

Basim went on to tell me about a driver who had taken over the job as Muhammad Ibrahim's chauffeur after Basim had been arrested. "And Muhammad Ibrahim has a younger brother," he added, almost as an afterthought.

That I knew. There were a total of nine Al-Muslit brothers in that branch of the clan. I had identified them all in the process of putting together the link diagram. "Which one?" I snapped.

"Sulwan," he replied. "I see him sometimes at the food market."

"What does he do there?"

"He buys food, mister. Lots of food." Basim answered as if the information was irrelevant.

"What does he do with it?"

"He loads it in his truck and heads out of town."

"Where out of town?"

"Over the bridge to the east."

"Basim, who is Sulwan buying that food for?"

Now it was his eyes that were fixed on me. "Maybe he is buying food for Saddam, mister," he said.

✳ ✳ ✳

I had been going at Basim for six hours. We all needed a break. I rushed back to the house to find Kelly and Bam Bam. They needed to know what I had learned as soon as possible. The insurgency network that we'd been painstakingly tracking had suddenly broken wide open. We had to make our move before the window of opportunity closed again.

"Muhammad Ibrahim is running the whole thing," I told them as we sat down at the dining room table. "The whole insurgency is under his control."

"All of Tikrit?" Kelly asked in disbelief.

"No," I replied. "All of Iraq."

I gave them a moment to absorb the information. While Bam Bam sat calm and collected as usual, Kelly got up and returned a moment later with a copy of our link diagram.

"Okay," he said, taking out his pen. "Let's go over this step by step. Who is Muhammad Ibrahim working for?"

"Saddam."

Once again there was a long silence. "Basim told you that?" Kelly said at last.

"Yeah. He's got leaders in different regions, but Muhammad Ibrahim's giving the orders. And paying the bills. Basim used to carry around hundreds of thousands of dollars in the trunk of his car."

"Who are the men under Muhammad Ibrahim?" Kelly asked, quickly sketching out new squares on the link diagram.

"One of them was Radman," I said.

"What was his territory?"

"Baghdad, Tikrit, and the west."

Kelly gave a low whistle. "That's quite a territory. Who else?"

I glanced at Bam Bam. He was listening intently, but it was hard to read his expression. I was unloading a lot of information that could save a lot of lives. Or turn out to be complete bullshit. It was going to be up to him to act on what I was telling him. "Farris Yasin, Muhammad Ibrahim's cousin, was in charge of Kirkuk. And there was a guy named Abu Sofian who was running the operation in Samarra. He's dead now, but Basim is sure they've found a replacement." There were a few other names Basim had given me that I passed along. Kelly assigned them places on the link diagram. When I was done, the three of us sat looking at the new chain of command. Bam Bam still hadn't said a word.

"So what's our next move?" Kelly asked.

"I think we need to go after Thamir Al-Asi," I replied. I knew that Bam Bam had previously turned down a hit on the cement store owner. Being a friend of Muhammad Ibrahim wasn't grounds enough to arrest him. But I hoped now that things were different. We were getting closer and I could feel the unspoken excitement between the three of us.

"Why Thamir Al-Asi?" Kelly asked. He pointed to the link diagram. "We've got all these new targets now."

"But our main target is still Muhammad Ibrahim," I reminded him. "And Basim said he sleeps at Thamir's place."

" 'Sleeps,' as in sleeping there now?"

"I don't think so," I admitted. "Since Basim was first arrested a month ago he's lost contact with Muhammad Ibrahim. He's probably made changes to his daily routine to cover himself."

"So why are we hitting Thamir's place?"

"I don't think Muhammad Ibrahim has many options left, Kelly. Besides, I think Basim may be trying to protect Thamir. He keeps insisting that Muhammad Ibrahim wouldn't be there anymore. I say we find out for ourselves." I stopped abruptly, realizing I'd overstepped my bounds. This wasn't my decision to make. Kelly and I turned to Bam Bam, the only person at the table whose opinion really mattered. I saw something on his face I'd never seen before. A smile. "We'll hit him, we'll hit them all," he said in an unnervingly calm voice. "Anyone else we need to go after?"

I could hardly believe what I was hearing. Bam Bam wasn't just approving a hit that he had previously rejected. He was letting me know, in his own quiet way, that he trusted what I was telling him, that I had gained his confidence. His decision to arrest Basim had been a huge risk. But it was beginning to pay off. He was ready to take it to the next level.

So was I. I swallowed hard and answered his question. "Well, since you asked," I said jokingly, "Basim can also take us to Muhammad Ibrahim's father-in-law. That's where his wife is staying with their three-month-old baby. He also knows about his old boss's favorite hooker. He might be hiding at her place. And there's a driver who took over from Basim after he was arrested. I'd go after all of them."

Bam Bam thought for a minute. "Forget the father-in-law," he said. "I don't want to hear about some stray round killing a baby, especially since we know the baby's in the house. But if I were on the run, I might hide with a hooker. Besides, he probably thinks we wouldn't dare hit a woman's house." That made sense. As much as possible, coalition forces in Iraq tried to keep women out of danger. We never arrested them or used them as sources. It would have gone against every moral code in the culture and would have been useless anyway. Arab women would never dare speak out against their men.

In the end Bam Bam decided to go after four targets: the locations of Thamir Al-Asi, the hooker, Muhammad Ibrahim's new driver, and, for good measure, another random Al-Muslit brother whom Basim had talked about during our interrogation. The 4th ID would handle the hits on the brother and the driver. Our team would go after Thamir Al-Asi and the hooker. The raids were set for midnight the following evening.

CHAPTER 13

AMIR

0045 03DEC2003

It was early morning, December 3 and the simultaneous raids were under way. I went to find Kelly in the communications room to wait for the status reports.

As the minutes ticked by, the tension mounted. There was a lot riding on these hits, not the least of which was the validity of my theory that Muhammad Ibrahim and his cronies were directing the entire insurgency, working directly under Saddam's command. I needed to bring him in, and the targets that Bam Bam had approved were my best shots at pinning him down. It all depended on where Muhammad Ibrahim decided to sleep that night. If he was in Tikrit, I had a pretty good feeling it would be at one of the locations we had targeted.

Since both the team from the house and the 4th ID's unit had been thoroughly briefed on where to go and who to look for, it wasn't deemed necessary for me to go on any of the hits. Instead I would stay back, waiting to begin the interrogations as soon as any detainees were brought in. At the last minute, the 4th ID was also given the mission of raiding a farm to look for another Al-Muslit brother. Bam Bam wanted to cast as wide a net as possible.

At about 0130 words started coming in. Thamir Al-Asi had been at his house along with his two sons. No Muhammad Ibrahim. The Al-Muslit brother had been at home with his wife. No Muhammad Ibrahim. At the farm there had only been hired hands. No Muhammad Ibrahim. At the house of the driver, only the driver's elderly parents. No Muhammad Ibrahim. And finally, the hooker was at home, sleeping alone. No Muhammad Ibrahim. Five hits. Five dry holes. It was not shaping up to be a good night.

Worse still, each raid was producing exactly what you'd expect to find if you raided the houses of completely innocent people: frightened and bewildered people who had no idea what you were looking for. All we had accomplished was awakening a bunch of innocent bystanders. By early morning it was clear that, unless we came up with another target, the whole night would have been wasted. At that point, Bam Bam made the decision to raid the cement store of Thamir Al-Asi, where Basim had told me that Muhammad Ibrahim often came to play dominoes with his friends. Since it was already daylight and there were likely to be other people in and around the store, he wanted me in on the raid. It would be my job to separate out anyone we might want to talk to from everyone else.

The cement store hit was scheduled for later that morning, so I decided to briefly question Thamir and his sons, who had been detained and brought back to the guesthouse. As much as anything, I wanted to find out what we could expect to uncover at the cement store.

My initial questioning didn't yield much. Thamir Al-Asi was an old man who seemed completely disoriented by having been dragged out of bed in the middle of the night. But he wasn't so confused that he didn't know what to lie about. He insisted that he hadn't seen Muhammad Ibrahim since the war started in April. I knew better. Both Basim and Abu Drees's son had put the insurgent leader in Thamir's house or at the store within the past few weeks. But that was his story and he was sticking to it.

So were his sons. Actually, the younger kid was a college freshman who was on semester break and had come home for a visit. I believed him when he told me he had no clue what I was after. The older son was another story. His name was Amir and he actually worked in the cement store. Not that it made any difference. He swore that he hadn't seen Muhammad Ibrahim in four months and had never actually talked to him at all. On top of that, I couldn't get either the old man or his older son to admit to having ever played a game of dominoes with the former bodyguard. I was getting nowhere. I left the Al-Asi family at the guesthouse to think things over and got ready for the hit.

The cement store was no more than three minutes from the front gate. As we drove out, I reflected on the fact that Muhammad Ibrahim had once been sitting with his friends not more than a half mile away from me. I could only hope that something would turn up this time.

It was 0800 when we arrived and a few people were already on the street, doing their morning chores. The shooters went in first, knocking down the front door and swarming into the cramped space. I followed and, taking a look around, saw nothing but stacks of cement sacks and a bag of Iraqi dinars worth about $500. The team moved upstairs where there were a few more shops on the second story. A moment later they came down with a white-haired old man, almost toothless and squinting at the bright light from the broken door.

"We found this guy upstairs," one of the operators told me. "He says he's the security guard for this place." I laughed. It was as much to relieve my frustration as it was at the thought that this old guy could guard anything.

"Who owns this cement store?" I asked and my terp had to shout the question just so the guard could hear it.

"Thamir Al-Asi and Muhammad Ibrahim," he muttered.

"When was the last time you saw Muhammad Ibrahim?"

"Three days ago." I had the terp repeat the question, just to make sure I was getting an accurate translation from him.

"Where was he?"

"Here," the old man answered. "He plays dominoes with his friends."

"Which friends?"

"I don't remember their names."

"Thamir Al-Asi?"

"Yes, of course. He runs the store. I saw him here three days ago."

"Basim Latif?"

"Who is that?"

"Muhammad Ibrahim's driver."

"Yes. He was here three days ago as well."

"Abu Drees?"

Yes. Three days ago."

I was beginning to wonder if the old guy knew what he was saying. Everyone I asked him about had been in the cement store three days ago. The only problem was that Abu Drees and Basim Latif had been in our custody for considerably longer. But at the very least, I had something else to go back and confront Thamir Al-Asi and his son with.

＊ ＊ ＊

It had been an exhausting twelve hours. We had raided virtually every place in Tikrit where Muhammad Ibrahim might
have been and came up with nothing. The harder I searched
for this guy, the more elusive he became. It had been almost
a month now since Radman Ibrahim's son had given me the
names of Muhammad Ibrahim's three closest friends: Basim
Latif, Abu Drees, and Thamir Al-Asi. We now had all three of
them in custody and I had interrogated each of them. But we
were no closer to our quarry than when we had begun. I was
running out of people to question and places to look. I had no
other choice but to go back to square one and try to dig out
more information from the prisoners. Maybe there was something I missed.

I decided to focus on Thamir Al-Asi's older son, Amir. He
worked in the cement store and had admitted to at least seeing
Muhammad Ibrahim there. Maybe there was a chance I could
get him to admit something else. It was worth a shot.

After an hour of listening to Amir insisting on his complete
innocence, I slowly and carefully explained to him that I basically didn't care. His father was a close friend of Muhammad
Ibrahim. I knew that for certain from the information I'd already gathered. I didn't need him to either confirm or deny the
fact. His father's house and place of business had already been
hit. I showed him the bag of dinars we'd found in the cement
store to prove the point. Muhammad Ibrahim hadn't been at
either location. So where was he?

Amir emphatically denied knowing anything about his father's activities or his connection to Muhammad Ibrahim.

"That's not the point," I countered. "You're in trouble

because of what you know. You know things you're not telling me and you know things I just told you."

He gave me a puzzled look.

"Amir," I explained, "I just gave you everything we've learned about Muhammad Ibrahim. That's dangerous knowledge. If I let you go, you could take it back to the bad guys. What I've told you makes you valuable to them. I couldn't let you go free now even if I wanted to. You'll be staying with us until we find who we're after."

"But they won't look for me," he cried. "I am nobody."

"That may be," I said reasonably. "And maybe your brother is a nobody, too."

At the mention of his younger brother, the college student Ahmed, Amir stiffened. He obviously wanted to keep him out of trouble. It was a concern I could exploit.

"Your brother seems like a nice kid," I continued. "He's probably going to make something of himself. But if I bring him in here and tell him everything I'm telling you, then we'll have to hang on to him, too. On the other hand, I know he wants to help you and your father any way he can. He's a good son and a loyal brother. Maybe I should send him out to track down Muhammad Ibrahim on his own. Of course, if the insurgents found out who he was working for, that might make him a liability."

"He knows nothing," Amir insisted. "He had been away at school for many months."

"I believe you," I replied. "But, as I said, I don't give a shit. I need Muhammad Ibrahim and I'll do what it takes to get him. You tell me where he is and I'll let you and your brother and your father go. Otherwise, none of you will ever get home again."

Amir glared at me but kept silent. I sensed that he was a smart and practical kid. He was ready to crack. All he needed was a little more incentive. I had an idea and called for the guard to bring Basim in from the other room where he was being held.

Amir looked shocked to see his father's old friend walk through the door. I took advantage of the moment and moved quickly. "Basim," I said, "talk to this fool and tell him to cooperate with me."

Basim sat down in a chair next to Amir. "What is the problem?" he asked in a calm and measured voice. "Just tell him what he wants to know, Amir."

"But I don't know anything," the kid repeated with a desperate look in his eye. The arrival of Basim had definitely shaken his self-confidence.

With a nod to me, Basim took over the interrogation, as the terp translated their conversation for me. "You are in big trouble, Amir," he said. "There is no way for you to leave here without telling this man everything he wants to know. I have already told him everything. Now you must do the same."

Amir's fear turned to something like relief. He was depending on Basim now to guide him through the process.

"Don't fuck with me, Amir," I said, moving in close. I knew he was about to break and I needed to give him one last push. "This is your chance to help your father and your brother. Your only chance."

He looked at me and Basim and back again. He took a deep breath and let it out. "Mister," he said, his voice trembling, "they run everything out of my father's store. All the attacks. My father couldn't stop them. Muhammad Ibrahim owns the store. He can do as he wishes."

"So he operates the insurgency from your father's place?" He nodded numbly. "And who comes to see him at the store?"

"Everyone," Amir admitted. "His brothers and his cousins."

"What are their names?"

"I don't know." He turned to Basim. "Ask him. He knows them all."

Basim looked as if he'd been kicked in the front of the shorts and threw Amir a dirty look. "Muhammad Ibrahim is not in Tikrit anymore," he said scowling. "Tell him."

Amir nodded. "He left when Basim was arrested, a month ago."

"Where is he now?" I pressed. Amir was silent. "Look," I said in my most persuasive tone of voice. "What has Muhammad Ibrahim ever done for you? He's the reason you and your dad and maybe even your brother might spend the rest of your lives in prison. Why are you protecting him?"

That seemed to get through. The kid straightened in his chair. "I have seen him driving into town."

"With who?"

"A man from Samarra."

"What man?"

"The brother of Abu Sofian."

I quickly scanned the link diagram I had embedded in my mind. Abu Sofian was the Samarra insurgent leader who Basim had acted so proud to know. He had died a few weeks earlier. "What's the name of Abu Sofian's brother?"

"Muhammad Khudayr," Amir replied. I shot a quick glance at Basim. He looked as if this was all news to him.

"Where does he live?" I asked Amir.

"In Samarra," he told me. "Close to the parents of Sabah. I don't know exactly where."

New names were coming at me quickly now. Muhammad Khudayr was the brother of a known insurgent, seen in the company of Muhammad Ibrahim. But who was this Sabah? I turned to Basim.

"Sabah also works for Muhammad Ibrahim," he told me. "He came often to the cement store to get money for their operations in Samarra."

"I delivered cement to the house of Sabah's parents," Amir said. Basim started talking to Amir, trying to figure out which house in Samarra he had delivered the cement to. Then the driver turned to me.

"I know Sabah's parents," he said. "If you take me to their house I can show you where Muhammad Khudayr lives. It is very close."

I liked the way this was going. For the moment, the three of us were working together, unraveling the connections that might lead to Muhammad Ibrahim. It certainly wasn't standard procedure to have one prisoner talking with another, but I'd given up standard procedure a long time ago.

"Is Muhammad Ibrahim in Samarra?" I asked, returning to the primary objective.

"I don't know," Amir replied. "But I know that his brother Sulwan Ibrahim has rented a house there."

Sulwan was another of Muhammad Ibrahim's brothers, the one Basim had seen buying quantities of food at the market, food that was possibly meant to feed Saddam. Suddenly, from the utter failure of the previous night, I had all sorts of new directions to follow. The random list of names and places I had kept in my head for so long were beginning to link up and intertwine. I was drawing in, tighter and tighter.

"This rental house," I continued. "Where is it?"

"I don't know," Amir replied. "But Muhammad Khudayr will know."

I backed up and replayed what I had just learned. Amir could take me to the location in Samarra where the parents of the insurgent operative Sabah lived. From there Basim could locate the nearby house of Muhammad Khudayr, the brother of the late Abu Sofian, another insurgent commander. Khudayr, in turn, might be able to take us to a house rented by Sulwan, the brother of Muhammad Ibrahim. It was a complex and challenging task. But it was also the last best hope I had of accomplishing our mission.

I got Amir to draw as exact a map as possible of the Samarra neighborhood where Sabah's parents lived, and Basim showed me the proximity of Muhammad Khudayr's house. Then I went back to deliver this major data dump to Kelly and Bam Bam.

This time Bam Bam didn't need more than a minute to make his decision. "We'll take Basim and the kid to show us the Sabah house this afternoon," he told us. "Then we'll hit it tomorrow along with Khudayr's place." He turned to me. "Muhammad Khudayr is going to take us to Sulwan's rental house, right, Eric?"

I nodded a lot more confidently than I felt.

"I'll hold you to that," he replied, and left to get the preparations for the upcoming hits under way.

"That sure was easy," I said to Kelly. Up until this point, it had been almost impossible to get a hit approved based solely on intelligence gained from an interrogation. But events were moving quickly now and Bam Bam had proved his readiness to stay out in front of the curve. We were all invested now in reaching the goal we had worked so hard to achieve.

"We need to turn up something fast," Kelly told me. "The situation with Basim and the security chief is going to get serious sooner than later. And all those raids we did yesterday came up with exactly nothing. Tomorrow night needs to pay off. It may be the last shot we have at this thing."

"Let me ask you something, Kelly," I said, almost afraid to hear his answer. "Do you think we're getting closer to Muhammad Ibrahim?"

"It doesn't matter what I think," he responded. "We've got to come up with something to justify what we've been doing all this time. We pissed off our Sunni friends, and have a link diagram full of names nobody's heard of outside of this house. Our asses are on the line, bud."

CHAPTER 14

1.9

1815 04DEC2003

Basim and Amir went with the team to Samarra to recon the Sabah house for the raid the following night. The two had become
quite a team. When we had finished our questioning for the day,
I left them alone, removing their handcuffs and supplying them
with cigarettes. I wanted them to talk together, to get comfortable with each other and accustomed to the idea of cooperating
with me. There was an element of mutual motivation that was
working to my advantage. The two of them could share information, filling in the blanks in each other's knowledge. At the
same time, I was hoping they would see that only by working
together could they achieve their freedom.

I didn't try to win them over by being overly polite or ac-
commodating. I was just honest. I had explained the situation
they were in and how they could improve it. I made it clear that
I would do everything I could to help them out because, by gain-
ing their cooperation, I was furthering my mission. We needed
each other and that, in turn, created a strange kind of friendship
that would last as long as our mutual dependency existed.

But at the same time, I never fooled myself into thinking they were actually on our side. I had, for instance, debated whether to take Amir's father, Thamir Al-Asi, and Amir's younger brother back to the 4th ID prison. I had no further use for them at that point. But I quickly decided that I needed to keep them around to remind Amir why it was a good idea to continue working with me. They would remain at the guesthouse.

On the evening of the raid, my two prisoners and I stayed up talking for almost four hours. I finally suggested that we all try to get some sleep. It was going to be a big night.

"No," Basim insisted. "I will start a fresh pot of tea. We need to keep working."

Amir agreed. "If we are ever going to get out of here, there are many more things you need to know."

I smiled to myself. You know a detainee is completely broken when he insists on continuing an interrogation session.

And I needed all the help I could get. By December 6, the morning of the Samarra raid, my tour of duty in Tikrit was winding down. No one had actually given me a date for my departure and I wasn't about to bring it up. But I was pretty sure I'd be hearing from Baghdad within a few days at the most.

The idea of leaving before the mission had been accomplished was unthinkable—I couldn't just pack up and move on before I had seen this thing through. I was the one who had put Bam Bam, Kelly, and the rest of the team on the line in the first place and I was convinced that we were closing in on something very big and very real. Muhammad Ibrahim was running the insurgency in Iraq under orders from Saddam Hussein. That meant he was in direct contact with Black List #1. If we captured him, he wouldn't necessarily reveal where Saddam was hiding, but taking him down would be like cutting off Saddam's right hand.

As night fell I did my best to get Basim and Amir ready for the hit. Since life inside the guesthouse was dull and uneventful, Basim had initially been excited by the prospect of a real combat raid. But as the hours wore on, I could see him getting progressively more nervous. I wanted them both to stay focused and, above all, to understand how much was riding on the success of these hits. If we found Muhammad Ibrahim, I guaranteed them they'd be released within forty-eight hours. But if we came up with more dry holes, their future prospects would become a lot more problematic.

So would mine. I could probably serve out the rest of my enlistment in the Army and go back to civilian life knowing that I tried my best. But how was I going to live with the realization that my best wasn't good enough?

★ ★ ★

It was 0030 on December 6 when the Samarra raids got under way. Once again Kelly and I were waiting in the communications room for word to come in over the radio. It seemed to take forever. Finally, at 0100, we got word that the team had kicked down the door where Sabah's parents lived. An hour later Bam Bam made his first report.

"Dry hole at first objective," he told us. My heart sank. "We are moving on second objective."

Confused, Kelly and I looked at each other. Did that mean they were moving on the Muhammad Khudayr location?

"Confirm location of second objective," Kelly requested.

"We're going to the rental house," Bam Bam replied.

"Thank you, God," I whispered. Whatever had happened at the Sabah hit, it had given them enough information to locate

Sulwan Ibrahim's rental house. But if they hadn't rolled up anyone at the first hit, how did they know where to go now?

Ten minutes later Bam Bam called in to report that the rental house was being assaulted. We waited tensely for another thirty minutes before we heard the results.

"Dry hole at second objective," Bam Bam said, his voice betraying no emotion. "RTB, with two PAKs." RTB was "Return To Base." PAKs were prisoners. The raids were over, and sitting in that cramped room crammed with communication gear, I felt totally confused. What just happened? We hadn't found our targets, but they were returning with two prisoners. It seemed like we'd reached another dead end. Was Muhammad Ibrahim real or was I chasing a ghost? I could find his buddies, his driver, his business partner, everybody but the man himself. My time was almost up. So were my options.

The team arrived just as the sun was coming up and the two new detainees were brought in for processing. The first was a guy named Luay, the brother of the Samarra insurgent leader Sabah. He'd been the only adult male at his parents' house at the time of the raid. Luay was the one who had revealed the location of the rental house to the shooters. Since it seemed more likely that Muhammad Ibrahim would be hiding there, Bam Bam had made a quick decision to skip Muhammad Khudayr's house and go directly to the new location. There they had captured Muhammad Ibrahim's eighteen-year-old son, whose full name was Muslit Muhammad Ibrahim Omar Al-Muslit.

I began to breathe a little easier. The raid hadn't been a total failure. We had actually found the rental house and rolled up the son of our prime objective. I was still in the game.

Before I started interrogating my new charges, I checked in with Basim to get his perspective on the night's events. I could tell as soon as he walked in the room that he had something on his mind. I asked him what was wrong.

"I will tell you what is wrong," he snapped back. "They did not go to Muhammad Khudayr's house. I know Muhammad Ibrahim was there and we did not go to get him."

I was caught off guard by Basim's agitation. It surprised me to see him so invested in the raid's success. Of course, he had everything to gain from the capture of his old boss. But right then, it seemed as if he was really rooting for our side. I realized that, in spite of myself, I kind of liked Basim.

"What about this guy we got at the Sabah location?" I asked, trying to calm him down. "Is it Sabah's brother?"

He nodded. "Yes. I have seen him before, but I don't know him."

"I need to talk to him now, Basim," I continued. "But if he doesn't cooperate I may need your help."

"You won't need my help," Basim assured me. "You will make him talk."

"What makes you so sure?" I couldn't resist asking.

He grinned. "I wasn't going to tell you anything, and look what you have gotten out of me."

I headed over to the room where Luay was being held. As usual I started with the preliminary questions establishing his background. But before I could get too far into it, I got a call from Kelly.

"You might want to come over here," he said.

Shit, I thought. What now? "Am I in trouble?" I asked.

"Just get your ass over here," Kelly replied. "There's something you should know before you start interrogating Sabah's brother."

I went back to the house and entered through the kitchen door. There I was stopped dead in my tracks. Kelly and the team were standing at the table, where neatly piled bundles of hundred-dollar bills had been stacked in an impressive pyramid. It was more money than I had ever seen in my life. Hell, it was more money than any of us, put together, had seen.

"Thought you might like to know what 1.9 million dollars looks like, Eric," Kelly said with a huge grin.

I just stared. "Where did it come from?" I asked at last.

"After we hit the Sabah place, we were in a hurry to get to the rental house," one of the shooters explained. "We just piled everything we could find into the Humvees and headed out. We got a safe that we didn't open until we got back." He gestured toward the money. "That's where we found this."

"We needed this," I said, turning to Kelly. "I hope it means we can keep going now."

"You just bought us 1.9 million dollars' worth of time," he replied.

"How long is that?"

"Longer than we had a few hours ago."

I headed back to the guesthouse, feeling great, talking to myself, and not caring who might be listening. "We ain't done yet," I said out loud. "Are we done, Casey? Hell no, we ain't done, brother. We're just getting started." With $1.9 million, my theory suddenly had a lot more credibility. More important, it went a long way toward justifying what we'd been doing in Tikrit since the team arrived. We were obviously after the right guys, with the means to finance and carry out the insurgency. We'd proved that much. Now all we had to do was find them.

★ ★ ★

I was reenergized and on the top of my game when I continued my interrogation with Sabah's brother, Luay. I was ready to work all day to get anything and everything he knew. But I didn't have to. He collapsed like a house of cards within five minutes.

While falling short of an outright admission that his brother was a terrorist, Luay did acknowledge that the nearly $2 million we had found was used to fund the insurgency. Muhammad Ibrahim, he said, had given it to his brother Sabah as a slush fund for the Samarra operation. Luay also revealed that he had sat in on several meetings between his brother and Muhammad Ibrahim, as well as Abu Sofian, before the coalition forces had killed him. The whole crew would drink tea as they planned out attacks and reported on their latest recruits.

But it didn't take me long to realize that Luay wasn't cut out to be a real insurgent himself. He didn't have the nerve for it. He was much more interested in his upcoming wedding, he told me. It was scheduled to be held in four days. He admitted with a shy smile that he was a virgin and that all he wanted was to make it to the mosque on time. No global war on terror was going to keep him from his future wife. He would do and say whatever necessary to get his detainment over with as quickly as possible.

After a couple of hours I called in my new backups, Basim and Amir. More than anything, I wanted to see how Luay would react. Maybe he had something more to tell that their presence might shake loose. He did, in fact, look stunned and surprised when they walked in, and he began talking even faster than he had before.

"My brother Sabah left for Baghdad three days ago," he said before I'd even had a chance to ask the question. "I haven't seen them since. I haven't seen any of them since."

"How often did you see them before that?"

"Almost every day. Sometimes they would stay and talk. But usually they just picked up Sabah and left."

"Where did they go?"

"I don't know. They would leave at night and Sabah would come back in the morning."

I moved in closer, wanting him to understand that his answer to my next question was crucial. "How often did you see Sulwan?" So far, Sulwan, Muhammad Ibrahim's brother, was my most direct link to Saddam. It was Basim who had seen him buying large amounts of food in the market.

"I saw him a lot with Muhammad Ibrahim," he replied. "He would come to the house. But only during the day."

"Why only in the day?"

He shrugged. "He would leave in the evening. I never saw him at night."

"Where did he go?"

"I never asked." I looked over at Basim. He was obviously thinking the same thing I was: Sulwan was going to Saddam's hiding place at night.

"Did Sulwan stay at the house he rented in Samarra?" I continued.

"No," he replied. "I don't think he stayed in Samarra."

"Then why did he rent the house?"

"It was for Muhammad Ibrahim. After Basim was arrested he couldn't stay in Tikrit anymore." He glanced over at the driver. "Muhammad Ibrahim was certain you were working for the Americans."

"Do you know who this is?" I asked, changing tack and pointing to Amir. I was curious how familiar the Samarra insurgency was with Thamir Al-Asi and his sons.

"Yes," Luay replied. "That is Amir Thamir Al-Asi. He shouldn't be here. He has done nothing."

"Just answer the questions, asshole," I shot back. "You

haven't earned the right to an opinion yet. Only Basim has earned that right." The driver laughed. Giving him his props was the right thing do. I wouldn't have come this far without his cooperation, willing or otherwise.

I'd gotten as much out of Luay as I could, at least for the moment. It was time to move on to the next prisoner. "I'm going to talk to Muhammad Ibrahim's son now," I told Basim, Amir, and Luay. "You want to hang around and listen?" Once again, I was going against interrogation doctrine, but letting prisoners talk to each other had served me well so far and I was curious what might come up if the three of them were on hand.

But they weren't interested. In fact, they seemed terrified at the prospect of even meeting the kid.

"If he knows we are helping you, our families are dead," Basim explained on behalf of the others. "He may be just a boy, but his father is very powerful. We cannot be seen by him."

"No problem," I replied. I glanced over at Luay. He had tried his best to help. Maybe he'd be useful later. I turned back to Basim and Amir. "What do you say, guys?" I asked them. "Want another roommate?"

They agreed and the three of them were escorted out. Luay would get his own cot, a share of the cigarettes, and a chance to spend some time with his new best friends. I wished I could have been a fly on the wall for their rap sessions.

★ ★ ★

Muslit Muhammad Ibrahim Omar Al-Muslit was a pretty pathetic specimen. The son of a high government official, he'd obviously been pampered and protected his whole life. It was hard to imagine that his father was a ruthless insurgency leader. Muslit was scared of his own shadow.

I started off the questioning slowly and reasonably. I was just trying to get a feel for whom I was dealing with. It didn't take long. He naturally insisted that he knew nothing about Muhammad Ibrahim's activities. But I actually felt sorry for him when he explained why.

"My father is embarrassed that I am his son," he told me. "He would never trust me with any important information."

"What kind of information would that be?" I asked, trying to determine exactly what he did or didn't know.

He sank lower in his chair, as if he wanted to disappear completely. "He is hiding from the Americans," he said sorrowfully. "If he told me where he was, he is afraid I would tell you."

"Would you tell me?"

"Even if I could, I have nothing to tell."

"I'll decide that," I replied. "How long had you been at the house where we found you?"

"Only three weeks. No more."

"Where were you living before you moved to Samarra?"

"On my uncle Sulwan's farm in Kirkuk." That was another location I needed to look into. The kid knew more than he thought.

"Why did you leave?" I continued.

"My uncle was nervous. He thought he was being spied on."

"Had you ever been to Samarra before?"

"We used to go fishing here. When I was little, my father would take me to the river."

"You don't go anymore?"

He shook his head and gave me a forlorn look. "My father hates me."

Muslit was breaking my heart. "Do you miss fishing with your dad?"

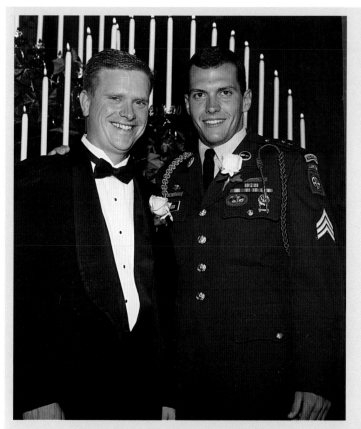

At the wedding of my lifelong friend Ryan Ritchie in 1997. Ritchie and his wife, Kara, are the godparents of my younger son, Eric Marshall Maddox.

(Private collection of Eric Maddox)

The famous deck of cards listing High Value Targets and distributed to U.S. forces in Iraq. These cards were signed by seven former regime members, including Chemical Ali.

(Private collection of Eric Maddox)

The palace similar to the one that served as
our base of operations in Tikrit.

(Patrick Robert/Corbis)

One of the few Tigris River bridges in Tikrit. Insurgents posted lookouts here to spot U.S. military traveling east, toward Saddam's hideout.

(AFP/Getty Images)

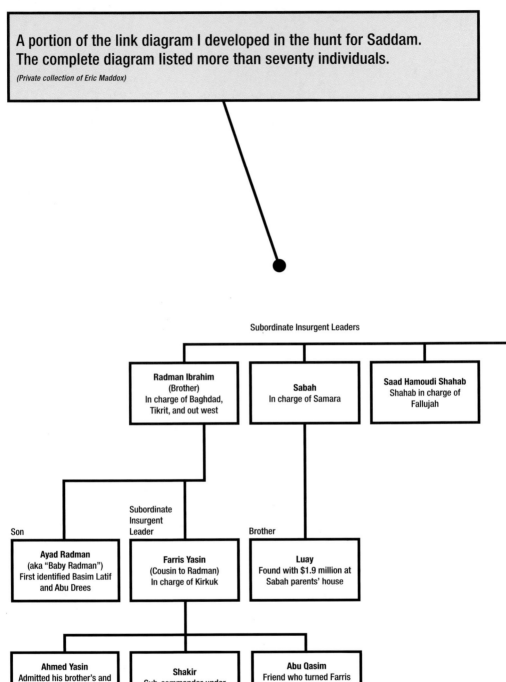

A portion of the link diagram I developed in the hunt for Saddam. The complete diagram listed more than seventy individuals.

(Private collection of Eric Maddox)

Subordinate Insurgent Leaders

Radman Ibrahim
(Brother)
In charge of Baghdad, Tikrit, and out west

Sabah
In charge of Samara

Saad Hamoudi Shahab
Shahab in charge of Fallujah

Son

Subordinate Insurgent Leader

Brother

Ayad Radman
(aka "Baby Radman")
First identified Basim Latif and Abu Drees

Farris Yasin
(Cousin to Radman)
In charge of Kirkuk

Luay
Found with $1.9 million at Sabah parents' house

Ahmed Yasin
Admitted his brother's and cousin's involvement in the insurgency of October

Shakir
Sub-commander under Farris Yasin in insurgency

Abu Qasim
Friend who turned Farris Yasin in via his grandson on 11/7/2003

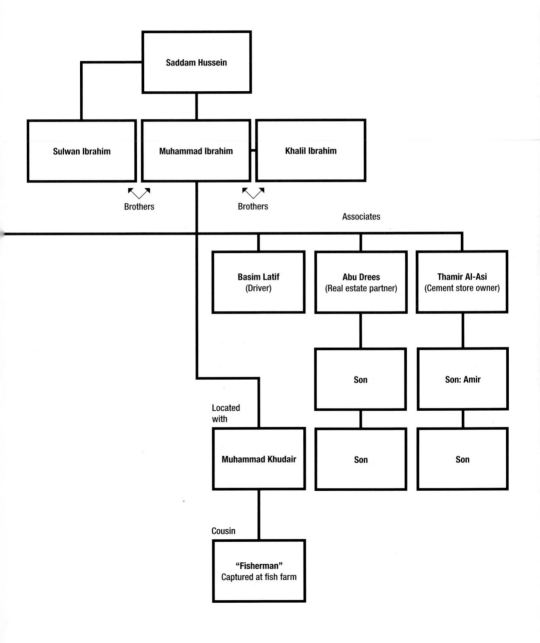

Posing (in the blue shirt I wore for virtually my whole tour of duty) for a final photo with my fellow interrogator Lee *(right)* and his interpreter John *(center)* on December 13, just hours before leaving Iraq.

(Private collection of Eric Maddox)

The infamous spider hole. This tiny cramped dugout was where the dictator was finally run to ground.

(AFP/Getty Images)

A defeated and demoralized Saddam, in a photo taken on December 14, 2003, just a few hours after his capture.

(epa/Corbis)

A cigar found in Saddam's Tikrit spider hole and presented to me by the team who captured him. I had it mounted and framed.

(Private collection of Eric Maddox)

Director of Central Intelligence Agency Porter Goss presents me with the National Intelligence Medal of Achievement for my role in the capture of Saddam.

(Private collection of Eric Maddox)

The Legion of Merit. I was deeply honored to receive this award, which is rarely given to non-commissioned officers.

(Private collection of Eric Maddox)

"Yes," he replied sorrowfully. "He still fishes at his pond in Samarra. But he never asks me to go with him anymore."

"How often does he go fishing?"

"He is there all the time." This was getting interesting. I had another place on my list of Muhammad Ibrahim's hangouts. I continued questioning in the same quiet, measured tone. I was encouraging him to reveal more about his troubled relationship with his dad. There was a lot of information between the lines.

"When was the last time you saw your father?" I asked.

"He was at the house two hours before your soldiers came," he said.

"What?" I could hardly believe my ears. But it was obvious the kid wasn't lying. He didn't have it in him to be deceptive. Muhammad Ibrahim had been at Sulwan's rental house. If we'd gotten there two hours earlier we could have rolled him up. As frustrating as this information was, it was also gratifying to know that we had been on the right track. Bam Bam's decision to go directly to the rental house had been correct. We just got there too late.

"When was the last time Sulwan was there?" I continued.

"He was also there that evening. He left right before dinner as he usually does."

"Where does he go?"

The kid shrugged.

"Does you father still live there?"

"Sometimes. Sometimes he goes to another place. I don't know where it is. He doesn't take me with him."

"Do you know when he's going to be there again?"

Muslit shook his head. "He would never tell me such a thing."

"When was the last time your father was there before last night?"

"He was gone for three days. He came home in the afternoon and left in the evening."

"What car did he use?"

"He was picked up. By Abu Sofian's brother. His name is Muhammad Khudayr."

"Where did they go?"

"I think to Muhammad Khudayr's house." I thought back to Basim's insistence that our target for last night had been at that exact location. It was time for a consultation. I left Muslit and went back to the room where my three homeboys were bunking.

"Hey, Basim," I told the driver as I came through the door. "Maybe you were right. Muhammad Ibrahim may have been at Khudayr's place last night."

"Of course he was," Basim replied smugly.

"Okay," I continued. "So I'll give you that one. Tell me where he is now."

Basim shrugged. "He could be anywhere. At a hotel or an abandoned building or maybe at another relative's house."

I thought for a moment. "What did he do for relaxation when he was in Samarra?" I asked.

"He went fishing," Luay chimed in, wanting to be helpful. It was confirmation of what Muslit had just told me: that his dad was an avid fisherman.

"Where does he go?" I asked Luay.

"They have a fish pond," he replied. "Muhammad Ibrahim and Muhammad Khudayr own it together. They have stocked it with fish from the river. The pond is right next to the river."

"Have you ever been there?" I asked, turning to Basim.

He nodded. "They go there all the time. I have driven them. They fish and drink whiskey."

That pissed me off. "Why didn't you tell me that before?" I demanded.

"You didn't ask," he replied, grinning. "Mister, my brain doesn't work like yours, but if you ask me I will tell you what I know." It was hard to stay mad at the guy.

"So where is this pond?"

"It's behind Muhammad Khudayr's house," Basim explained. "There's a dirt road there. You can follow it for about five kilometers and you will see it. There is a little shack by the shore."

"You think they might be hiding there?"

"Sure," Basim replied. "Hiding from their wives."

The three of them had a good laugh. Then Amir looked me straight in the eye, put his hands on my shoulders. "I know this pond," he said. "My father has been there many times. It is their sanctuary. You will find them there. I am sure of it."

I didn't need any more guarantees. It made sense. There was a curfew in effect across the entire region. If Muhammad Ibrahim had left the rental house last night he wouldn't have gone far. He had to be somewhere close by to avoid the roadblocks and patrols. An isolated fishing hole outside of town sounded about right. And I was ready to cash in on the credibility that $1.9 million had earned the team.

"We missed Muhammad Ibrahim by two hours," I told Kelly as soon as I got back to the house to brief him. I wanted to start out with fresh intelligence before I made my pitch for another raid.

I watched as the same emotions I'd experienced crossed Kelly's face: frustration, followed by the elated realization that we were hot on the trail of the bodyguard. "So what's our next move?" he asked.

"Kelly, we need to do another raid." As exasperation clouded his expression, I hurried on before he could object. "Just listen for a minute. Muhammad Ibrahim was staying at his brother Sulwan's rental house in Samarra. Sulwan doesn't stay at that house. He goes somewhere else, almost every night. Where does he go?"

"You tell me," Kelly answered skeptically.

I plowed on. "Basim told me that he has seen Sulwan at the market buying quantities of food. Who's that food for, Kelly?"

"Get to the point, Eric," he snapped.

"All right," I said. "I think that Sulwan is taking that food out to Saddam. I think he stays the night there to guard him and comes back in the morning."

There was a pause. "So where is he?" Kelly asked at last. "Where's Saddam?"

"Wait," I pleaded. "Just hear me out. Remember that I told you how Saddam is partial to a certain kind of fish, prepared a certain way?"

"Yeah," he answered. "I remember. Mazgoof, wasn't it?"

"Very impressive memory," I joked before getting back to business. "So suppose you're a dictator who is used to having whatever you want, whenever you want it. Are you going to go without your daily serving of Long John Silver's?"

"What are you getting at, Eric?" Kelly was losing patience fast.

It was time for the payoff. "Muslit, Muhammad Ibrahim's son, told me that he used to fish with his father. They don't do it anymore, but that's another story. Muhammad Ibrahim likes fishing so much that he bought a pond with Muhammad Khudayr and stocked it with fish. They've even got a little cabin out there. Fish, Kelly. You see where this is going?"

"You want to raid a fish farm?"

"Does that sound crazy?"

He thought for a moment. "Not any crazier than any of the other shit you've told me. I'm just glad we found that money. That's going to give us some clout when we try to sell this raid."

"What happened to all that cash?" I asked.

"We're going to hand it over to Civil Affairs. The 4th ID is due to pick it up, and Bam Bam will brief them on how we found it."

"Why?"

"Because they're going to take credit for it," Kelly explained. "They'll have a press conference and may even take the reporters out to the site. They get the glory and we stay under the radar. That's the way we like it."

I laughed. "And the way they like it, too. Pretty soon they'll start believing it themselves."

"It's not their fault. We asked them to do it." He stood up. "Come on. Let's see if we can get a hit on this fish farm."

We found Bam Bam sitting with the rest of the shooters in the dining room. As Kelly and I started to brief him, they all stopped what they were doing to listen in. An eerie silence fell over the place. At that moment, we were all thinking the same thing: there might actually be a shot at rolling up Saddam. No one said as much, but you could feel it in the air. I think Bam Bam felt it, too. He agreed immediately to raid the fish farm that night.

I had hoped to go on that hit. I was certain that this would be the one that would bring in Muhammad Ibrahim. I wanted to be on hand for the occasion, but it was also just part of my control freak nature. It was one of the hardest lessons I had to learn from my months in Tikrit. In a house full of Type A personalities, I wasn't the alpha dog. The fact was, I didn't need to be on the hit. They had already decided to take Luay as a guide, and I would have just been extra baggage. I had told the team everything I knew about the targets they were going after. Most of them had already studied the link diagram in detail. They had a good grasp on Muhammad Ibrahim and his network. They were totally up to speed.

In the hours before the raid, I hung out with Basim, Amir, and Luay. It wasn't an active interrogation, just a way of keeping the connection between us active. These three had been more help to me than most of the other detainees combined and we all had a vested interest now in seeing this through.

Joining us that afternoon were all the terps who I had come to depend on over the past several weeks. Jimmy, Samir, and Jafar had learned to function like a well-oiled machine, trading off sessions with one another and even working together to make sure the translations were accurate. As the days and weeks of intense work had progressed, I had moved from the main house to a cot in the guesthouse. The terps settled in there, too, making sure one of them was available day or night. It wasn't a requirement of the job, but I think as time went on they had begun to realize that Muhammad Ibrahim was a key figure in the insurgency that was tearing their country apart. They wanted to be a part of the effort to bring him in, and they realized how important to the mission they were.

As evening fell, I could smell the aroma of steaks being cooked on a makeshift barbecue grill the team had set up on the front porch. Cookouts were a regular part of the routine.

I rounded up my three terps and took them with me for dinner. I found myself wishing I could bring the three roommates, too, but they were still prisoners. Regardless of how much I might have liked those guys, that was one barrier that couldn't be crossed.

As I sat eating my meal, Kelly came over to run down the plan for the night. "We're going back to hit Muhammad Khudayr's house," he told me. "But they're going to send the team up from Baghdad for the fish farm."

That wasn't the best news I'd heard all day. The Baghdad shooters didn't know the situation and the players like our guys. "Why do we need them?" I asked. "We can hit them both."

"The money caught the attention of the brass back at Baghdad," Kelly explained. "Now they want to play."

"But—" I began before Kelly cut me off.

"Look, Eric," he said. "It's fine. These are our operators who are coming up. This way we can hit both targets at the same time and we don't have to get the 4th ID involved. The place is easy to find. It's not going to be a problem."

"So when is TOT?" I asked, referring to time on target.

"0100," he replied. "We're only going to have a couple of hours at the objectives. Samarra is a hot spot. Bam Bam wants to get in and out. We'll hit the Khudayr target either way. But we're going to wait for someone to show up at the pond before we go in."

"How will you know when someone's there?" I asked.

"We've got eyes on it," he replied. Kelly was referring to orbiting military satellites that had focused on the exact coordinates of the fish farm and were transmitting imagery as we spoke. I didn't have time to think about the wonders of modern technology. I was too focused on what was about to go down.

So was Kelly. "Since we found that money, we're in good shape," he said to me. "That was terrorist cash and everyone knows it. But, Eric, the way I see it, this could be our last shot. I don't really know where we go after this."

"I don't know where we go either," I admitted.

"You haven't got any locations still hidden up your sleeve, do you?" he asked, only half joking. He knew as well as I did that any information I got was only as good as the detainee or source who had given it to me. If tonight's hits were dry holes, I seriously doubted whether the three guys I was depending on back at the guesthouse would have any more good ideas. Kelly was right. This could be our last shot.

★ ★ ★

The team headed out for Samarra around midnight. I watched them leave then headed back to the house to wait for the OU football game to get under way. It was an important one: the Big Twelve championship. So far the Sooners had played an undefeated season and, in my humble opinion, had emerged as the greatest college team of all time. They were about to prove it again by whipping the Kansas State Wildcats. I was one hundred percent certain.

I was feeling pretty good. We were on our way to pick up Muhammad Ibrahim, the man who I was sure could lead us to Saddam himself. And OU was going to finish the season in true style by dismantling the Wildcats. It didn't get any better than that.

Within the first ten minutes of the game, OU had jumped out to a 7–0 lead. Can of corn, I thought to myself and went to check in with Kelly. He was in the communications room as usual, checking the surveillance monitors on the fish farm. "Want to watch?" he asked as I came in.

I sat down next to him. On the screen was live infrared coverage of the target area around the pond and the nearby river. It was clear enough to get a good idea of what was happening on the ground. After watching the empty landscape for about twenty minutes, we both saw the same thing at the same time: two figures emerging from the darkness. We sat bolt upright as they went to the water's edge, climbed into a boat, and paddled into the pond. It had to be the two Muhammads—Muhammad Ibrahim and Muhammad Khudayr, right where they were supposed to be.

Kelly made a quick call to Walt, his analyst counterpart in Baghdad. "They're in the pond," he told them. "I can see them right now."

"I don't see anything," Walt replied. "We're not going to move until we have a fix on them."

Kelly swore and slammed down the phone.

"What's going on?" I asked.

"I think they're watching a different monitoring system," he told me.

"So what?" I didn't have time to think about the glitches of modern technology. This was going down in real time.

"So if they can't see it on their channel, then it doesn't exist."

"Of course it exists," I shot back, pointing to the image on the screen. "There's a boat with two men in it."

"You see it and I see it," Kelly replied grimly, "but if they don't see it, they aren't going to do the raid."

"Look, Kelly," I said desperately. I was talking fast now, trying to think of some way, any way, to make this happen.

"These guys know that we only conduct raids after midnight. They can stay in their houses until then. After that they have to find someplace else to hide. Those fishermen in that boat didn't show up until after midnight. Don't you see? They're hiding on the river. They fish for a couple of hours until it's safe to come back. Most of our hits are over by 0300. You can catch a lot of fish in that time, to make a lot of mazgoof."

Even while I was talking, trying to convince myself and Kelly, the report from Bam Bam came in. Muhammad Khudayr's house was a bone dry hole. There wasn't a single adult male at the place. The fact that many of the women found there were the wives and widows of insurgency leaders, including the spouses of Sulwan, Sabah, and Abu Sofian, did us absolutely no good. We weren't about to spark an international incident by bringing women in for interrogation. The night's prospects were quickly turning to shit. I had to think of something. "Kelly," I said, inspired by my desperation. "Let's get Bam Bam to do the hit on the fish farm right now."

He shook his head. "They're running out of night," he told me, looking at his watch. It was coming up on 0300. "We'll have to wait until Bam Bam gets back and talk it over with him then."

"By then they'll be gone," I told him, looking at the glowing images of the fishermen. But even as I said it, I realized it was hopeless. There was nothing Kelly could do. Bam Bam had made it clear that all operations in a place as dangerous as Samarra had to be done under cover of night. The last thing anyone wanted was another Mogadishu.

Once more it looked like Muhammad Ibrahim had slipped away. All I had to even prove he existed was a faint heat trace on a computer screen. Exhausted I sat alone at the dining room table. I thought I could never feel as discouraged I as did right then. But that was before I checked the score of the OU–Kansas State game. The Sooners had been taken apart. Their chances for the championship were all but over.

CHAPTER 15

OUT OF TIME

0445 07DEC2003

Bam Bam was crystal clear: we wouldn't be going back to the fish farm that night. I knew that he had as much at stake as any of us in seeing the mission succeed. But he was too good of a leader to let his emotions get in the way.

That doesn't mean I didn't do my best to talk him into it. "The two Muhammads are at the fish farm," I pleaded with him. "I'm one hundred percent certain." Kelly shot me a dirty look. We all remembered what happened the last time I made a confident prediction based on percentages. But this time Kelly actually agreed. "We've still got a couple of hours before daylight," he said. "If we went now we could be in and out before morning. We could just grab whoever's there and head back."

"We can go tomorrow," Bam Bam answered calmly. "We have no assets or support from Baghdad. They agreed to go on this raid and we can't afford to piss them off."

Kelly and I should have known enough to back off. But I could feel everything we worked for so long and hard slipping away. We couldn't let that happen. "As soon as we started going after Muhammad Ibrahim in Tikrit, he went to Samarra," I said. "Now, since we did the hit on Muhammad Khudayr's, he knows we've followed him there. He's sure to make a run for somewhere else and this time we may not be able to figure out where he went. This may be the last time he's even in this area."

Bam Bam didn't budge. "First of all, we don't know for sure it's him out at that pond. Second, if it was him, he obviously feels safe there. If it's him, he'll probably come back. We'll do the hit tomorrow." He picked up his gear and just before he went upstairs he turned to me and asked, "How did the Sooners do tonight?" He either didn't know they'd got beaten or it was his way of sending me a message. Earlier that day I had guaranteed an OU victory over Kansas State. That didn't happen. Maybe I didn't always know what I was talking about. Maybe I was wrong about the raid, too.

All I could think about were those two infrared silhouettes on the computer screen. Even if we got lucky and managed to find Muhammad Ibrahim at the fish farm again, I would still be facing the challenge of getting him to talk. Over these past few weeks, we had staked everything on the capture of this one man. And there was only one thing worth getting from him: the location of Saddam.

Having dealt with so many of Muhammad Ibrahim's inner circle, I knew the intense loyalty they had for him. Abu Drees, Thamir Al-Asi, Farris Yasin: these men had been difficult, if not impossible, to break. What would I be letting myself in for when I came up against their leader? Could I even get him to acknowledge that he was a terrorist, much less that he was taking his orders from Saddam? I had wished more than anything else to be able to find Muhammad Ibrahim. In those early morning hours, tossing and turning in my cot, I reminded myself to be careful what I wished for.

★ ★ ★

The second raid on the fish farm got under way at 0200 the next day. From the start, it looked like we might get a break. Just like the night before, the two fishermen appeared in the surveillance monitor and launched from the shore in their dinghy. This time Baghdad saw it on their system, too. Kelly and I resisted the temptation to get on the radio and tell them I told you so.

After a half hour, the two men rowed back to shore and headed for the fishing shack with their catch. This was almost too easy. There was no place for them to go, no place left to run. We had them cornered. As Kelly and I watched on the screen, the shooters rushed in and secured the location. The radio crackled to life. Two PAKs had been detained. Kelly and I looked at each other. Congratulations were in order—almost.

Then, after a tense twenty-minute wait, another message came through: a dry hole. They were bringing in some detainees, but not the ones we were after.

No way! I thought to myself as I sank back into my chair. Kelly just stared at the computer, a stunned look on his face. Was this the punch line to some kind of sick joke? I had been given every resource available to complete this mission. The men I was honored to work with were the best soldiers in the world, and they were led by an aggressive and courageous commander under whom it had been my distinct privilege to serve. We had a top-notch analyst, a team of dedicated interpreters, and even three prisoners who had worked tirelessly for us. And yet we still couldn't get this son-of-a-bitch. Was he ever even at the fish farm? Was he ever anywhere? Did he even exist?

I felt like I was losing my mind, but I had to pull myself together. I turned to Kelly. "What do you want me to do now?" I asked.

He continued staring at the screen. "I wanted to wait to tell you this," he said at last in a voice barely above a whisper. "Baghdad called earlier. You need to catch the next flight back. I could have kept you here if we'd found Muhammad Ibrahim, but it doesn't look like that happened. You're going home. There's a helicopter due in at 2100 Monday night. You're supposed to be on it." He looked at his watch. "They're picking you up in seventeen hours, Eric."

So that was it. My time in Tikrit had officially come to an end. I felt numb. My worst expectations had come to pass. I was leaving without completing my mission. I had interrogated hundreds of prisoners; interviewed scores of informants; wracked my brain to break open the insurgent network that was wreaking havoc on the country; worked endless hours and talked myself hoarse. And it was all for nothing. In seventeen hours I'd be gone and none of it would have made any real difference.

It was time to go back to the guesthouse and start packing my gear. I stood up. "Is there anyone else we need to be looking for?" Kelly asked me as I walked to the door.

"I don't have anything right now," I replied in a hollow voice. "I'm sorry."

Kelly did his best to raise my spirits. "I'll have photos of the two PAKs from the fish farm sent up here," he told me. "It's probably a good idea to have Basim and the boys take a look at them. Who knows, we may have one of the two Muhammads without knowing it."

I doubted it. The shooters knew our targets. My misgivings were confirmed a couple of hours later when Kelly brought the digital mug shots in. I showed them to the Basim, Amir, and Luay but none of them recognized the men captured at the fish pond.

I couldn't help it. I vented my frustration on the three prisoners, focusing my anger on Basim. "Look at the fucking pictures again, you asshole," I shouted. "You think these guys just decided to show up and fish two nights in a row? Who the hell are they?"

They looked at the photos, then back to me, each with the same helpless expression on their face. I think they were just as confused and discouraged as I was. I took a deep breath and tried to calm down. What was my next move?

Obviously I needed to talk to the two detainees who had been rolled up at the fish farm. The only problem was, I didn't have access to them. Since we had found the money, Baghdad's interest and involvement had disrupted the smooth-running interrogation system we had established. The prisoners had been taken back to BIAP. They'd be questioned there.

I put in a call to Lee, my old friend who was still stationed at the Baghdad airport. I had had occasional conversations with him over the last five months. But I hadn't seen him since that day in late July when I hopped a chopper ride to Tikrit. On a secure Army line I asked him now to check on the status of the two detainees and to let me know as soon as he found out who they were and what they had been doing at the pond.

A few hours later he called me back. "Hey, brother," he said. "Those two fishermen you were asking about? They're just fishermen."

"Did you question them yourself, Lee?"

"No," he replied. "I'm not in charge around here anymore. All the interrogators get randomly assigned. But I talked to the guy who questioned them. He seems pretty sure they're just a couple of civilians. It's pretty crowded down here, Eric. We don't have a lot of time or space to waste. They want to let these guys go as soon as possible."

"Lee," I begged, "I'm coming up there tonight. Can you hold on to them for that long? I really need to talk to those guys."

"I'll do my best," he replied. I think he could hear the strain in my voice. "But if you have anything on them, tell me what it is. That will make it easy to keep them around for a while."

"I've got nothing," I admitted. "They were supposed to be two different targets. Muhammad Ibrahim and Muhammad Khudayr."

There was silence on the other end of the line. "Never heard of them," Lee said at last. "And my guess is, nobody else up here has either. Who are they?"

"It's a long story," I sighed. "Just please make sure you hang on to those fishermen as long as you can. I'll take responsibility for them as soon as I get there."

"Consider it done, brother."

I hung up. Talking with Lee had given me an idea. If Baghdad wasn't going to let me stay in Tikrit, maybe I could take Tikrit with me to Baghdad. I went to find Kelly.

"Look," I told him as we sat together at the dining room table. "I have to leave tonight. You'll be left here with all these prisoners we've rounded up over the last few weeks. Why don't I take them to Baghdad with me? I'll be there for a couple of days. Maybe I can get something out of those fishermen." What I left unsaid was that I also wanted to have Basim and a few others on hand when I talked to the fishermen. Now that I understood the value of using one prisoner against another, I didn't want to give it up.

"Which ones do you need?" Kelly asked me.

"Basim," I said immediately.

"What about Thamir Al-Asi's son, Amir?"

"No," I replied. "I think we should cut the kid loose. He's just trying to survive. Let's give him a break."

"And Luay?"

I thought for a moment. "He sat in on all those meetings with Muhammad Ibrahim. We found him in the house with all that money. He may still have something more to tell us. Besides, he's highly motivated. He's supposed to get his cherry popped in two days."

"As long as you're at it," Kelly said, "why don't you take Abu Drees and Thamir Al-Asi? We could use a little more room in the prison."

I shrugged. "I'll take them all, Kelly."

"Then I'll get the approval," he said. There was a long pause. We both knew that this was the end of the line for our working relationship. We had been thrown together in an uncertain and unpromising situation and, through it, become a team. I'd asked him to take some real risks and he'd backed me up when it counted. We had accomplished a lot. But we hadn't finished the job. It was a realization we both shared as we sat one last time at the table where we had spent so many hours together.

I reached over and slapped him on the back. "It was great to work with you, Kelly," I said.

He looked over and smiled. "Dude, you're gay," was all he said.

It was getting dark by the time I stood at the helicopter pad with a motley crew of prisoners waiting for the flight back to

Baghdad. We must have made an odd sight: one guy in a faded blue shirt with a duffel bag escorting a gang of handcuffed prisoners ranging from a teenager to an old man. It was like I was bringing back souvenirs from my stay in Tikrit.

I'd already said my good-byes to the shooters. If they were sorry to see me go, they didn't exactly show it. I expected as much. They were consummate professionals trained to not show emotion. I'm sure they liked me well enough and had even come to respect the work that I did. But for them, Tikrit was just another mission in a war that brought people together and pulled them apart with no regard to friendship. They didn't get too close to anybody except each other. They were an elite fraternity I would never be a part of. I accepted that. I was just grateful that they had let me be a part of their world for a little while.

As I waited for my ride, a figure came out of the dusk to see me off. It was Bam Bam. "We gave them a run for their money," he said, as the lights of the chopper appeared in the distance. "We were really close to getting this thing done and we know that. You worked hard. Don't think that wasn't appreciated."

"Thanks, Bam Bam," I said as we shook hands. Whatever else might have been said between us was lost in the roar of the descending chopper. I climbed on board with the rest of my human cargo and watched as the ground shrank below me. I could see the guesthouse where I had spent so much time and effort and the lights from the kitchen where someone was preparing dinner. It had been my home for the last five months, the place where I learned a lot, about human nature and about myself. It had marked an important passage in my life, and the most significant mission of my career.

Sure, I thought as we peeled off to the east. We gave them a run for their money. But in the end, did any of it really matter?

CHAPTER 16

BACK TO BAGHDAD

2212 08DEC2003

We arrived at BIAP just after 2200 on Monday night, December 8. Lee was waiting at the runway with a truck. From the minute we saw each other, we just picked up where we had left off five months ago. He was my best friend and although we were glad to see each other, there was no need to express it in words.

With a raised eyebrow, Lee looked over the gang of prisoners. "Too attached to your new buddies to leave them behind?" he joked.

I laughed, but my mind was on something else. "You still have the fishermen?" I asked.

He nodded. "They're waiting for you. The interrogators who talked to them have got new guys to deal with. They're all yours."

"Can I get a terp?"

"Use mine," he offered. "He's the best one here."

After I handed off the detainees for in-processing, Lee introduced me to the other interrogators. The whole operation was completely different from Tikrit. There were six interrogators working on a tight schedule in a building specially modi-fied for the purpose. They were about to have what is called a shift change meeting and invited me to sit in. After five months of working on my own, it was hard to see the point of going around a table where every interrogator reported on what they had been doing for the last twelve hours. It felt like a waste of time, but I kept my opinion to myself.

One of the interrogators explained how he had spent the last three days trying to get a prisoner to sign a written confes-sion. He was convinced that a confession meant that his subject had been broken. I thought back to my own experience. If I had depended on signed confessions, I would have been sitting with a pile of paper and no actionable information. You know a pris-oner is broken when he tells you something you can use.

It was only then that I really began to fully appreciate how valuable my experience in Tikrit had been. I didn't have to waste a lot of time on paperwork, whether it was the signed confes-sions of detainees or regular reports on my interrogations. I didn't need to get approval on whom to question or how to do it. That being said, I never used violent or unethical means. I didn't need to. I had developed my own methods that produced real results.

It wasn't until 0100 that night that I finally got a chance to question the two captured fishermen. As anxious as I was to talk to the fishermen, I didn't have a lot of confidence that they would provide me with any new leads. And even if they did, I wasn't going to have time to follow them up before I had to head back to the States.

But by now I was used to grasping at straws. I questioned the fishermen separately and almost immediately picked up some interesting information.

The first prisoner we had rolled up at the pond claimed that he owned the fish farm. I knew that wasn't true, since I had already established that Muhammad Ibrahim and Muhammad Khudayr held the title. Why was this guy lying? It would have made more sense to say that he and his buddy were simply in the wrong place at the wrong time, out at night fishing for their supper. To insist that he actually owned the place was to put him directly in the loop.

My next move was to take the fisherman out of the room. While he was gone I had Basim brought in and sat him down in a back corner. When the prisoner was returned I made sure he faced me directly. Basim's face remained in the shadows. I wanted him to hear the fisherman's story and give me his take.

I had the prisoner repeat everything he had told me and then outline his family connections and other background information. After about an hour he was escorted out again.

"This man is known for being the very best cook of mazgoof," Basim told me as soon as we were alone. "I have eaten his fish before. Muhammad Ibrahim uses him often to cook for his friends."

So the fisherman knew Muhammad Ibrahim. It seemed likely that he was trying to hide that information from me by claiming to run the fish farm instead of admitting that he knew who actually owned the place. What I needed to find out now was the nature of the link between my prisoner and the man I had been chasing for so long.

I had the second fisherman brought in. Basim remained in the shadows at the back of the room. I was thankful I'd decided to bring him to Baghdad with me. He had proven his value in a dozen different ways.

Almost from the start of my interrogation, it was clear that

the second fisherman had little to offer. Basim immediately signaled to me that he had no idea who the man was. But as I had
already learned in Tikrit, innocent bystanders could reveal a lot
if you ask them the right questions.

"How long have you been fishing with your friend?" I asked
him.

"About a month," he replied promptly. "We fish together
many nights."

"How did you meet him?"

"My brother. He said this man was looking for someone to
do work for him. I needed a job."

"What was your job?"

"Fishing."

"Does your boss own the fish farm?"

"I don't know," he replied. I believed him. He wasn't acting
as if he had anything to hide. "I think it was given to him."

"By who?"

"His cousin died last month. I think his family gave it to
him then. But I don't know for sure, mister. I just work for this
man. I swear I have done nothing wrong."

"Shut up," I ordered him. "I'll let you know if you've done
something wrong." I was thinking and I didn't want to be interrupted. Who had recently died? Radman Ibrahim Al-Muslit, Muhammad Ibrahim's brother, had keeled over from a heart attack
while in custody in early November. But I knew the entire Al-
Muslit family tree and this guy wasn't on it. Who else? Abu Sofian,
the Samarra insurgent leader and brother of Muhammad Khudayr,
had been killed a month earlier by coalition forces. Was it possible
that the first fisherman was related to Muhammad Khudayr?

I sent the second fisherman out of the room and ran my
theory past Basim. "It is most certainly possible," he told me.

That was all I needed to hear. I had the first fisherman, whom I now suspected was a relative of Muhammad Khudayr's, brought back in.

I started in on him again, taking into account my new theory. My aim was to get him to admit a connection to the two Muhammads.

"How long have you lived in Samarra?" I asked.

"My whole life."

"How long have you owned the fish farm?"

"For only a month."

"How did you get it?"

"It was given to me by my mother's family."

"Who gave it to you?"

"My mother's brother. My uncle. He is dead."

I glared at him. "If he's dead, how could he give you the fish farm?"

"It was his son," he stammered. "My cousin. He is dead, too."

I almost laughed. Did this guy hear dead people? "Listen, asshole," I shouted. "I want the name of someone alive. Who gave you the pond?"

He was quaking now. "My cousin," he told me at last. "He has a business partner. He gave me the pond."

"What is your cousin's name? The one who's still alive."

"Muhammad," he said in a voice barely above a whisper.

"Muhammad what?" I demanded.

"Muhammad Khudayr."

Now we were getting somewhere. I bent down in front of the trembling fisherman until I was inches from his face. I dropped my voice until he had to strain to hear me. "I want you to look at me and listen very carefully," I said. "Do you know why you're here?"

"No," he replied. "I have done nothing."

I shook my head. "You have done something," I told him. "You have gotten involved with some very bad men. Do you know who those men are?"

"No." He couldn't look me in the eyes.

"They are your cousin Muhammad Khudayr and his business partner. Do you know the name of his business partner, the man who gave you the fish farm?" I wanted him to say it first. If I told him that I knew it was Muhammad Ibrahim, I'd be tipping my hand. He could deny it or pretend he never heard the name. I'd be chasing ghosts again. It was critical that it came directly from him.

"No," he said. "I do not know his name."

There was a knock at the door. Lee appeared and motioned for me to come out. I sent everyone back to their cells and joined Lee in the hallway. With him was a guy he introduced as Walt, an analyst and Kelly's Baghdad counterpart. I'd never met him, but I knew him by name. He was the one whose tracking system couldn't see the boat on the pond when we did the fish farm raid. Not that it mattered now. The targets I had insisted were the two Muhammads turned out to be two fishermen. But I still had no use for Walt. To me he represented another obstacle to completing the mission. I'm sure the feeling was mutual.

But my opinion was to quickly change. "Are you talking to those fishermen?" he asked in a thick southern accent after we shook hands.

I nodded. "One of them is Muhammad Khudayr's cousin, he is more than just a fisherman." I was curious to see if the name would mean anything to him.

It did. "Mind if I sit in on the interrogation?" he asked. He had obviously taken an interest in where this might go next.

"Kelly's been keeping me up to date on what's happening. I know you've been looking for Muhammad Ibrahim and I can understand why. I think he's the key to the whole insurgency."

My regard for Walt suddenly shot up. "I'm glad you think so," I said. "I get the feeling no one else around here has ever even heard of him."

"Kelly sent everything straight to me," Walt explained. "I've been keeping a pretty close eye on what you all have been doing in Tikrit."

"I'm scheduled to ship out of here in a couple of days," I said. "But I may still get something out of these fishermen. Especially Khudayr's cousin." I looked him the eye. I had nothing to lose now. "If I get a target, will you push to have it hit?"

Walt smiled. "All I can do is make a recommendation to the commander," he replied. "But he usually goes with what I suggest. Kelly told me that if anyone could get anything out of those two fishermen, it would be you. That's why I'm here."

"Let's get to work then," I said.

Aside from his knowledge and support of the work we'd been doing in Tikrit, Walt proved his worth in another way. He was a pretty good interrogator. As soon as we brought back Muhammad Khudayr's cousin, the two of us went at him fast and furious. It was as if Walt understood the urgency I was feeling as my final hours in Iraq ticked down. By the intensity and volume of our questioning, we made it clear to the fisherman that we were determined to get the answers we were after. When one of us slowed down, the other picked up the slack and the prisoner hardly had a chance to catch his breath.

It was still a good three hours before his story started to crack. At first, he insisted that Muhammad Khudayr was no more than a distant relation and that he had no idea who his business partner might be. I was still holding back on mentioning Muhammad Ibrahim. I wanted him to bring it up first.

But I was running out of time. I finally had no choice but to give him the name of the man I'd been desperately searching for. "Your cousin's partner is Muhammad Ibrahim, asshole," I shouted. "You know it and I know it. And here's something else I know. You're going to spend the rest of your life in prison for aiding and abetting a known terrorist. We tried to help you but you didn't want our help. Now it's too late."

That did the trick. The fisherman started talking. In fact, once he got started, it was hard to keep up with him. "Yes, mister," he admitted. "Now I remember. It was Muhammad Ibrahim. Ever since Muhammad Khudayr's brother, Abu Sofian, died, they are always together."

"Do they go to the fish farm?" Walk asked.

"Almost every day. But they never stay there."

"Where do they stay?" I asked.

"My cousin's house or the house Muhammad Ibrahim rented in Samarra."

We had already been down that road. It had ended in two dry holes. "Where else?" I demanded.

"I don't know," he insisted. "They have left Samarra."

"When?" interjected Walt.

"Four days ago," the fisherman answered. "That was the last time I saw them."

"Where did they go?" I pressed.

"They are always together," the prisoner replied, trying to avoid the question.

"I didn't ask you that, shithead," I shouted. "I asked you where they went."

He looked from Walt to me and back again. You could almost hear the gears turning in his head. He had reached the inevitable conclusion. There was no way out now but our way. "I swear I don't know," he began, and then took a deep breath. "But my cousin and I have an uncle in Baghdad. Perhaps they are there."

"Where is your uncle's house?" Walt asked.

The fisherman gave us the location. By now he was fully cooperative. His was the typical profile of a broken prisoner, going from evasive and defiant to ready, even anxious, to help. He had no objection when we informed him that he was going on a recon to point out the exact location of his uncle's place.

After we sent him back to his cell, Walt and I conferred. "I think this uncle's house is as good a target as we're going to get," I said.

"You think they really might be there?" Walt asked.

After everything that had gone down in the last forty-eight hours, the last thing I wanted was to make another bad call. "I don't know," I admitted. "But I think it's worth a shot." What I didn't say was that it was probably going to be the last shot, at least on my watch.

Walt nodded. "I'll run this by the commander. I'm pretty sure he'll go along with it. He's as aggressive as they come."

I paused, picking my next words carefully. "Thanks, Walt," I said sincerely. "You know, I always assumed you were kind of . . . a dick."

He laughed. "Same here," he replied. "I always assumed you were trying to get Kelly on your side and discredit our input on Tikrit."

That's because your Tikrit intelligence was always wrong, I wanted to tell him. But I figured I'd said enough. I needed his help. Whatever was going to happen from here on out was going to happen without me. I needed someone to finish the job.

★ ★ ★

But, as it turned out, my usefulness had not quite come to an end. Later that evening, as I was winding down from the intense session with the fisherman, Lee asked me to come down with him to the flight line. A recent raid had gathered some detainees and he wanted me to help get them in-processed.

As we were standing at the runway, waiting for the choppers to set down, a full-bird colonel approached. He was on a first-name basis with Lee and after a friendly greeting I was introduced.

"Staff Sergeant Maddox," Lee said, "this is Colonel Walker, the J-2." That was impressive. J-2 meant that the colonel was the senior intelligence officer for the entire task force. He outranked every other intelligence official, analyst, and interrogator in the task force. Theoretically, Colonel Walker would have known about every information gathering operation that the task force was involved in. But it didn't work that way. I knew from direct experience that intelligence gathered in Tikrit, for instance, pretty much stayed in Tikrit. The intent was to keep the decision making as local as possible. Kelly and other analysts elsewhere knew better than anyone what the situation was in their part of the country. They tried to keep oversight from task force headquarters to a minimum in order to avoid unnecessary interference. It was for that reason that I was not required to write lengthy reports of my work. It avoided complications.

But now that I was face-to-face with the man in charge of task force intelligence gathering, I was beginning to have second thoughts. He was obviously interested in what had been going on in Tikrit. And it was just as obvious that he was pretty far behind the curve.

"How long have you been up in Tikrit, Sergeant Maddox?" he asked me.

"Five months, sir," I replied.

"What have you been doing there?"

"Just trying to get rid of the bad guys, sir."

"Any luck?"

I paused. Could I even begin to explain how close we'd come? "We did all right, sir." I answered.

"How come I haven't seen any of your interrogation reports?" he continued.

I swallowed hard. "Sir," I answered, "I was told not to worry about writing them up."

"I don't know who told you that," he said, clearly irritated. "We need those reports. Especially after that pile of money you all found. Can you write up a quick summary of what you've been doing in Tikrit?"

"Certainly, sir," I responded. "But I don't know how clear a picture a written report might convey. It's a complicated situation. I do have a link diagram that I can provide. And I can brief anyone who might be interested."

"Excellent," Colonel Walker said. "When are you shipping out?"

"Sunday the fourteenth, sir."

"I'm having an analyst's meeting on Thursday. I'd like you to be there. And bring your link diagram."

The colonel left and, watching him disappear into the darkness, I turned to my friend. "Lee," I asked, "anyone ever want to know anything about Tikrit before we found that money?"

"Eric," he replied. "We're in Baghdad. We stay focused on Baghdad."

We stood in silence for a long moment. "Do you think Saddam is in Baghdad?" I finally asked.

"I have no idea," he replied. "Why? Do you think he's in Tikrit?"

I thought back once more on all the mistakes I had made and all the dry holes I had turned up. In spite of it all, there was a feeling I just couldn't shake. "Yeah," I said to Lee. "I think he is."

★ ★ ★

I arrived at the briefing room at 1400 to find about a dozen analysts and intelligence officers slumped in their chairs waiting for me. It was clear from the moment I walked in that this was the last place they wanted to be. I was an unknown interrogator from a provincial backwater whom no one believed had any further significance in the ongoing hunt for insurgents. Everyone in that room shared the belief that whatever was happening in Iraq was happening in Baghdad. Everything else was a waste of time. If it hadn't been for the presence of Colonel Walker in the front row, I doubt they would have bothered to show up at all.

Standing at the front of the room, I considered starting off by telling anyone who wasn't interested that as far as I was concerned, they could take off. But I wasn't running the show. Colonel Walker was, and he expected a full briefing with his whole staff in attendance. They were obligated to at least stay awake.

Taking a deep breath, I unveiled a blowup of the link diagram I had prepared the night before and launched into a rapid-fire summary of what I had learned over the last five months.

Muhammad Haddoushi and the Al-Muslits, Radman Ibrahim and Farris Yasin, Thamir Al-Asi and Abu Drees, Basim Latif and Baby Radman. As I spoke, I thought back on each one of them. It seemed as if I had spent half a lifetime trying to get inside their heads and discover their secrets. In some ways it seemed that I knew them better than my own friends and relatives. I had matched wits with them, confronted them in a contest of wills and pushed them, and myself, to the limit. Some had broken, some hadn't. Some had told me what I needed to know and some would go to their graves without betraying their loyalty. They were foot soldiers in a cause that a few of them were willing to die for. I couldn't help but acknowledge that reality, even if their cause meant the death of thousands of Americans and Iraqis. They were, in their way, dedicated men. In order to stop them I had to be just as dedicated.

I didn't realize how deeply I had entered their world until I tried to explain it to others. I had interrogated over three hundred people during my time in Tikrit. I had put everything I discovered, along with all the conjectures I had made, onto that link diagram. I knew every person on it, and what his connection was to every other person. I knew who had given me the information that had enabled me to fill in each square on that diagram. And I knew who I had cross-checked to confirm that information. The end result wasn't just a graph of bad guys; it was a four-dimensional map of the insurgency. I knew it like the back of my hand, like the streets of my hometown.

But even while I spoke, painstakingly reviewing the time line and the cast of characters, I couldn't get away from the fact that they had won and I had lost. For all my determination, Saddam was still at large. The most wanted man in Iraq had eluded me and had lived to fight another day. My only hope was that the men and women in front of me would somehow continue the search and complete the mission.

It didn't seem likely. It wasn't just their bored expressions that made the debriefing seem so pointless. It was the fact that, in all likelihood, by the end of the week most of the information I was presenting would be forgotten or lost. Even as I left Tikrit, I had hoped that I'd somehow manage to buy the team another week or two to continue the search for Muhammad Ibrahim. They were deployed there for another month, but after they left, everything that Bam Bam, Kelly, and I had in our heads would be gone forever. That was one of the hardest parts of going home. If the mission wasn't completed, the intelligence that someone else might be able to use to finish the job would be lost.

And that wasn't just true for our particular situation in Tikrit either. A lot of valuable information was simply carried inside the heads of the soldiers stationed everywhere when they returned home. It was true that some commanders had made a concerted effort to preserve intelligence and pass it on. But what usually happened was that incoming case officers and analysts opted to develop their own leads and sources. Every time there was a change of personnel, it was like having to invent the wheel all over again. What had come before, no matter how valuable, was often discarded or ignored. It would be even truer in my case. Why should anyone listen to an interrogator with some dumb theories about the insurgency that he hadn't been able to prove? Running through the link diagram, I might as well have been making it up on the spot. Of course, the $1.9 million added some credibility to what I was saying. But the bottom line was the same: Saddam was missing. And no one in that room seemed willing to follow the clues that I was laying out.

But it turned out that there was one person who had been

paying very close attention. After I had finished the briefing and the analysts had asked a few halfhearted questions, Colonel Walker took me aside. "That was impressive," he said and I felt a flicker of hope. Maybe I'd gotten through after all, and to someone whose opinion counted. "Tomorrow you're going to give the same briefing to Admiral McCraven. Do you know the admiral, Sergeant Maddox?"

"I know he is currently the task force commander, sir," I replied, not quite believing what I was hearing.

"That's right," Colonel Walker said.

I had never spoken to anyone before with a star on his epaulet. Now suddenly I was being asked to meet with the man who oversaw the most elite military unit in the world. My last days in Iraq had taken an unexpected turn. It wasn't over, I reminded myself, until it was over.

"In the meantime," the colonel continued, "I want you to sit down with an analyst and go over your link diagram in complete detail. I don't want to lose this information when you go home. Is that understood?"

"Yes, sir." Not only was it understood. It was deeply appreciated.

CHAPTER 17

THE ZONE

1150 11DEC2003

I was looking forward to briefing the head of the task force. If I could convince him that my theory of the insurgency leadership was right, maybe the work we had done in Tikrit would continue.

Colonel Walker's response had been encouraging. But I had my doubts that anyone else could really step into my role in the mission. It wasn't that I thought I was indispensable. What was indispensable was the information I had put together over the last five months. It didn't matter how many briefings I gave to analysts. There was no way I could effectively pass on that information on. Not in the time I had left.

I was still hoping to hear from Walt about the raid on Muhammad Khudayr's uncle's house in Baghdad. It seemed like this was the last best chance we would have of rolling up the two Muhammads. But by the morning of December 12, two days before I was scheduled to fly home, I had received no word from him. I knew that he understood the importance of capturing Muhammad Ibrahim. I just wasn't sure how committed he was to pushing for a hit that seemed like such a long shot.

The situation had changed radically since I left Tikrit. There the decision to go on a raid was made only by Bam Bam. It was based on his belief in the intelligence I provided. We had a great working relationship. There was no formal reprimand if a hit turned up a dry hole. But there was always the potential for other, more serious, consequences. If I sent the team out on too many bad hits, it would reflect on my reputation and credibility with the whole team. Maintaining their confidence had been one of my prime objectives.

It was different in Baghdad. Walt's request for a raid would have been one of many considered by his commander. Approval would be based on hard data, not the sort of instincts I had developed in Tikrit. It was out of my hands.

I arrived at the admiral's office a little before 1200 and a few minutes later Colonel Walker showed up. He had several copies of the link diagram with him and seemed nervous. I could understand why. As the chief intelligence officer for the task force, he was about to turn over the reins to a mere staff sergeant. If I didn't make a convincing case, it would be his ass on the line. I wasn't worried. I knew what I was talking about. I knew it better than anyone. And, despite all our setbacks, I still believed in my theory.

Admiral McCraven was a tall, thin man with a powerful presence. After he and Colonel Walker greeted each other, I was introduced. "Staff Sergeant Maddox is here to give you a briefing on the situation in Tikrit, sir," the colonel explained.

"Very good," said Admiral McCraven. "Staff Sergeant Maddox, you are an interrogator, is that correct?"

I was about to answer when Colonel Walker jumped in.

"Sir, Staff Sergeant Maddox has spent the better part of the last six months in Tikrit, living with the team up there. He and their analyst Kelly have built a link diagram based on the information he has gathered from detainees and sources. I believe you'll be very interested in what he has to say."

"Excellent," replied the admiral, turning to me. "Are you ready to proceed, Sergeant Maddox?"

"Yes, sir," I said. I could see Colonel Walker out of the corner of my eye. He was still unsure about handing the ball off to me. But I was calm. It didn't matter who was there. I could brief this link diagram to anyone at any time. I knew it like the back of my hand.

For the next fifty minutes I went into detail, emphasizing the points that I especially wanted the admiral to retain. I reminded him of the $1.9 million we had found. I explained that the money was intended to fund the insurgency not just in Tikrit, but across the whole country. If there was one thing I wanted the admiral to come away with, it was the name Muhammad Ibrahim. I summarized as much of the search for Muhammad Ibrahim as I thought the admiral could absorb in one briefing. By the time I was finished with the former bodyguard, he was worse than the Antichrist. "If we can catch him, he could lead us to Saddam," I said confidently.

I finished by telling him about my interrogation of the fisherman. "As the cousin of Muhammad Khudayr," I said, "I believe that this man can lead us to where Muhammad Ibrahim is hiding." If Walt couldn't sell the raid on this last target to his commander, maybe I could sell it directly to Admiral McCraven. It was worth a try.

My concluding words were met with a long silence. I couldn't help but wonder if I'd overstepped my bounds. The admiral stared at me as if he were trying to figure out whether I was completely full of shit. Colonel Walker held his breath. I think we were both wondering which option the admiral would choose next: throw us out of his office or thank us for our time and forget about the whole thing.

Neither of us was prepared for what happened next. The admiral looked at his watch and turned to the colonel. "I'm scheduled to fly to Dohar, Qatar, tomorrow, colonel," he said. "Staff Sergeant Maddox will be accompanying me on that flight." Then he looked at me. "Sergeant Maddox, I will be briefing General Custard, the J-2 for General Abizaid at CENTCOM, on the status of the situation. I don't have time to learn everything about this thing." He gestured to the link diagram on the table. "You will be briefing him on it. Is that clear?"

"Yes, sir."

Colonel Walker cleared his throat. "Sir, Sergeant Maddox is scheduled to redeploy on Sunday the fourteenth. I assume that will be no problem."

"None whatsoever," the admiral replied. "He can catch a civilian flight to the U.S. from Doha. I need CENTCOM to hear what he has to say." The meeting seemed to be coming to an end. But before it did, I had a request to make.

"Sir," I said, "I have a partner who arrived in the country with me. He's also scheduled to redeploy back to the States on Sunday. Would it be all right if he came to Doha with me so that we could return home together?"

"I don't think that's a problem," the admiral replied. I wondered how Lee would feel when he heard that the head of the task force had approved his travel plans. "Colonel Walker," the admiral continued, "I want to thank you for bringing this to my attention."

He shook my hand. "Staff Sergeant Maddox," he said sincerely, "I want to thank you for your hard work. It's sergeants like you who win wars and make officers like Colonel Walker and me look good."

From the moment we left the admiral's office, the colonel treated me as if we were best buddies. He even started calling me by my first name. It didn't matter that he got my first name wrong. What mattered was that Colonel Walker was on my side.

My first thought was to ask him to push for the raid on the target that Muhammad Khudayr's cousin had identified. But there was no way I could directly interfere with the decision-making process. Walt was the only one who could sell the raid. He had a connection with the team in Baghdad and they trusted him. Colonel Walker would not have been willing to pull rank and interfere with that relationship. And I wasn't about to ask. All I could do was hope that Walt was making a good case for the hit.

Meanwhile I hunted down Lee to give him the news. We were going to Doha and were flying there on Admiral McCraven's personal bird. I had to convince him that I wasn't bullshitting. We ended the day at a restaurant that had been opened at BIAP for U.S. personnel. It was surprisingly good and I tried my best to enjoy the food. But the fact that I was actually leaving was just beginning to sink in. One of the most significant parts of my life, professionally and personally, was coming to an end. Looking back, I was proud to have worked with so many dedicated men, especially the team in Tikrit. We had tried to stop bad men from doing bad things. We were part of the greater good and had come very close to accomplishing what we had set out to do. Unfortunately, by this time tomorrow I would be on a plane with Iraq far behind me. It wouldn't matter how close we had ever been to capturing our target, Black List #1. We'd tried and failed.

★ ★ ★

When I got back to my tent, I lay down and closed my eyes. But I knew it was pointless. I wasn't going to be able to sleep on my last night in Iraq.

I got up and headed over to the prison. It was where Lee and the rest of the interrogators were hanging out. I was looking for someone to talk to, but I had to be careful. Aside from Lee, the rest of these guys were going to be staying behind for weeks or months to come. The last thing they wanted to hear was somebody talking about what it felt like to be going home. It was just good to be around fellow interrogators. I sat down and picked up an old magazine.

After a few minutes, a major came in and spotted me. "Hey, Maddox," he said. "Now that they sent your fisherman out on a recon, does that mean we can get rid of him tomorrow?"

I sat bolt upright. "What recon?" I was fully alert now.

"You didn't hear?" he replied in a deliberately disinterested tone. "They took him out yesterday."

"Did they find the target?"

"Yeah. In fact, they're on the hit right now."

Suddenly we were back in the game. I had a whole new admiration for Walt. He had been willing to risk failure if it offered even the slightest possibility of accomplishing the mission. I had underestimated him and now, at the eleventh hour, he had come through.

The phone rang and one of the interrogators picked it up.

After a short conversation he called over to me. "Eric, you know someone named Muhammad Khudayr?"

I jumped up, feeling a huge surge of adrenaline. "Hell, yes, I know him. Why?"

"That was Walt on the phone," the interrogator replied. "They got Muhammad Khudayr and a few other guys. He said you'd know what he was talking about. They're bringing him in now."

"What about Muhammad Ibrahim?" I asked.

The major shrugged. "Walt said they didn't get him, only Muhammad Khudayr."

It was good news, but not what I'd been hoping for. If Muhammad Ibrahim had been at the target, Walt would have known. Muhammad Khudayr was my only link to the former bodyguard. But I was running out of time to follow up the lead. I had needed Muhammad Ibrahim to be at that house.

But one Muhammad was better than none at all. I turned to Lee. "You want to work tonight?" I asked him.

"Do I have a choice?" he replied with a grin. He nodded to the night shift interrogator. "We'll take the new detainees coming in."

I was finally going to interrogate Muhammad Khudayr. It was a name I had first heard from Thamir Al-Asi's son, who had identified him as the brother of the dead insurgent leader Abu Sofian. He was closer to Muhammad Ibrahim than anyone else on the link diagram. And Muhammad Ibrahim was one step away from Saddam himself. The two Muhammads weren't just ghosts or figments of my imagination any more. We had one of them. Now we just had to get the other one.

It was 0200 before the shooters showed up with the four new prisoners. They were hooded and handcuffed. Muhammad

Khudayr was one of them. The others were unknown. I immediately asked the team commander, but was told Muhammad Ibrahim was not at the site. The shooters had been given a photo of him. It was the same blurry black-and-white snapshot I had carried around in my wallet for weeks. They knew who they were looking for. But they hadn't found him.

I had only a few hours left to question Muhammad Khudayr. But despite the pressure, I felt calm and totally in control. I was in my own personal zone, a place of complete confidence and self-assurance. It's a strange sensation, almost an out-of-body experience, like a batter at the plate, when the ball is as big as a grapefruit and impossible to miss.

As I prepared for the interrogation, I realized that I had been in that zone for a while now. It had started in mid-October, when I had questioned Ahmed Yasin. He had verified that his family was heading up the insurgency. That key interrogation had confirmed my theory. It gave me the incentive to look for this specific family of bodyguards even when the official hunt was focused on High Value Targets. More important, it had given me the ability to intensely focus on my job. A really good interrogator can usually get one out of twenty-five detainees to break and provide actionable information. An average interrogator might get one out of a hundred. Now I only had one to break and one night to do it. I wasn't worried. I was in the zone.

0218 13DEC2003

On my way to the interrogation cell, I ran into Lee's terp John, with whom I would be working for the night.

"I thought you were leaving, Eric," he said as he hurried alongside me.

"I've still got six hours," I replied. "I'm really going to need your help, John."

"Of course." I could see he was picking up on my energy.

We got to the prison where Lee was handling the in-processing. I pulled him aside. "This is going to go fast," I told him. "I need you to get a few of the prisoners I brought with me from Tikrit. I might need their help."

"Give me the names," Lee replied. He had his game face on. "I'll have the guards round them up. They'll be sitting out in the hallway in three minutes."

"Will they be able to hear the interrogation from there?" I asked. I only wanted them in on the questioning when it suited my purpose.

"Don't worry about it," Lee assured me. "I'll have them wear earplugs. They won't hear a thing."

"Great." I told him who I wanted: my most reliable collaborators, Basim Latif and Sabah's brother Luay.

We headed for the cell where the detainees from the hit were being held, still handcuffed and hooded. The guard pointed out Muhammad Khudayr. John and I walked him to the interrogation room. It was coming up on 0400.

The last thing I wanted him to know was that I was in a hurry. I needed him to think that we could go on all night and day if necessary. I started, as usual, with the basics.

"What's your name?"

"Muhammad." From his first answer I knew that he wasn't going to cooperate willingly.

"Muhammad what?"

"Muhammad Khudayr."

"Where do you live?"

"I live at the house where your soldiers came to get me."

"How long have you lived there?"

"Since the fall of Baghdad."

"Where else do you live?"

"My family lives in Samarra. I visit them when I am not looking for work."

"How long have you lived in the Baghdad house?"

"About two months."

At that point I took a calculated risk. This game of cat and mouse was eating up time I couldn't afford. I had hoped to get a feel for whom I was dealing with and what he wanted to hide from me before getting to the important questions. But this was no ordinary interrogation. Muhammad Khudayr wasn't going to give me the time of day, much less the time I needed to break him. I was going to have to speed this up and to try something new, something I would come to think of as the "brutally honest" approach. I had no choice.

"Muhammad," I said, keeping my voice pitched low so that he had to work to hear me, "I want you to look at me and listen carefully. I know exactly who you are and what you have done. I have captured and questioned many people who have worked for you. They've told me everything. You have to stop thinking about how you're going to get out of this situation. You need to stop thinking about what you are and are not going to tell me. I am going to explain exactly what you need to do. The only way you can help yourself is to help me. And the only way you can help me is to tell me where I can find Muhammad Ibrahim Omar Al-Muslit."

He stared at me defiantly. "I do not know this person."

"Let's try this again," I said in the same measured tone. "I know that you are personally responsible for the deaths of many Americans and Iraqis in Samarra and Baghdad. I know that you work directly with Muhammad Ibrahim Omar Al-Muslit. I know that you have been with him constantly since your brother Abu Sofian was killed a month ago." I leaned forward. "I know everything you've done."

"I don't know the man you are looking for."

I stood up and motioned for the guards to take the prisoner to the back of the room and gag him. I ducked into the hallway, where Lee was waiting with the detainees from Tikrit. As he had promised, they were wearing earplugs. I blindfolded Luay, the brother of the Samarra insurgent leader Sabah, and brought him into the interrogation room. Sitting him in front of me, I removed his blindfold and earplugs. He hadn't seen or heard Muhammad Khudayr, who was watching from the back of the room. I was improvising now, hoping I could pull off this last-ditch attempt to break the prisoner.

"Luay," I asked, "how many meetings did you sit through with your brother and his group when they planned attacks to kill Americans?"

"Too many," he replied.

"When was the last one?"

"About two weeks ago."

"Who was at that meeting with your brother?"

"Muhammad Ibrahim and Muhammad Khudayr."

"Were they at every meeting?"

He nodded. "Yes."

"Turn around, Luay," I told him.

Fear flashed on his face when he realized we were not alone. He pivoted in his chair to see Muhammad Khudayr, gagged and glaring at him. He had witnessed Luay give incriminating information.

"Luay," I continued, "who is that man?"

"Muhammad Khudayr," he whispered.

I had Luay taken out of the room. He could barely walk on his shaking legs. I sat back down in front of the prisoner.

"Obviously Luay has been helping me," I continued, sarcastically stating the obvious. "Now that you know, I can't allow you to leave here. That would put his life in danger. There is only one thing you can do to change the situation. Tell me where to find Muhammad Ibrahim. If you do that, then I'll know you're on our side. Just like Luay." He needed to understand that I had him where I wanted him. If he tried to retaliate against Luay, I would let it be known that he had helped us capture Muhammad Ibrahim. If he did cooperate then he'd have a vested interest in keeping it a secret—a secret he would share with Luay. "Do I make myself clear?" I asked to drive the point home.

A long pause followed, as he thought over his shrinking options. "I have heard of Muhammad Ibrahim," he admitted at last. "But I do not know him."

I left the room again, this time returning with Muslit, Muhammad Ibrahim's son. He still had a hood over his head, but I lifted it just enough for Muhammad Khudayr to recognize his face. For the first time since the interrogation began, I could see his composure began to crack. I took Muslit away.

"I know you know who that is," I said when I returned. I paused for a minute, as if considering my own options. "Here's what I'm thinking," I continued. "I'm thinking that I'll bring Muslit back in here to have a look at you. Then I'll make sure that everyone gets the message that Muhammad Ibrahim's son is going to spend the next fifty years in prison because of information you provided. I wonder how that will affect Muhammad Ibrahim's feelings toward you?" The tactic was a long shot, but I was willing to try anything.

"Muhammad Ibrahim has no regard for his son," he spat back.

"Maybe you're right," I said. "But I wonder how he'd feel if he knew you sent his close friends to prison for the rest of their lives, too."

"What friends?" he asked almost involuntarily.

"Basim Latif, Thamir Al-Asi, Abu Drees. I have them all in custody. I can put them away forever, and get everyone to believe that it was because of you. Would you like me to bring them in here?"

He shook his head but said nothing. We were stalemated. And there was a clock ticking loudly in the back of my head. "Muhammad Khudayr," I said, trying another angle, "I know you are lying to me because you think I am unsure of my information. But you are wrong. I know everything about you. I know all the crimes you have committed. And I know that the only way you can escape punishment is to take me to Muhammad Ibrahim."

"If I take you to him, he will kill me." We were making progress, even if it was agonizingly slow. At the beginning of the interrogation, the prisoner had denied even knowing Muhammad Ibrahim. Now he was telling me how afraid he was of the man. His fear was well founded. If it were discovered that he was cooperating with us, his life and the life of his family would be in jeopardy. I needed to find a way to help him with that problem.

"I tell you what," I offered. "You take me to Muhammad Ibrahim and I'll make sure that everyone knows that Muslit, his son, was the one that helped capture him. He's scheduled to be shipped off to Guantánamo Bay in a few days. Once he's gone, we can blame it all on him. You'll be in the clear." This was pure bullshit. I had no idea what was going to happen to Muslit. Since he wasn't actively involved in the insurgency, my guess was that he would be released sooner or later. But I needed to convince Muhammad Khudayr that he would have a way to protect himself and his relatives from Muhammad Ibrahim's revenge.

"If that happened, he would kill his son," the prisoner replied. "He would find a way. He will kill anyone who betrays him."

"Tell me where he is," I urged. "And he won't be able to kill anybody. As long as he stays out there he is still a threat, even to your family, especially now that you have been arrested."

Muhammad Khudayr's face sagged and his shoulders slumped. I held my breath. I had seen those signs many times, just before a prisoner starts to break. "He was at my house," he replied in a tired voice.

"When?"

"Last night."

How could that be possible? How could we keep missing this guy? Either he was the luckiest bad guy in the world or I was the unluckiest interrogator.

Muhammad Khudayr turned to my terp John and spat out a string of Arabic. "Eric," John said slowly, "he is saying that Muhammad Ibrahim was at the house during the raid."

That just wasn't possible, I told myself. The shooters who had done the hit knew who he was. They had the same photo I had. They couldn't have missed one of the most wanted men in Iraq.

But they hadn't missed him. If what Muhammad Khudayr was telling was the truth, then we had actually gotten him.

My mind flashed to the other detainees that had been rounded up in the raid. I had assumed that Muhammad Khudayr was the only prize. Every stage of the hunt so far had been intricate and difficult. One capture led to another and then to another. We had always taken one painstaking step at a time. And it had always seemed that the bad guys were one step ahead of us. Was it possible that we had just taken a giant leap?

"Keep an eye on him," I said to John. I jumped up and bolted out of the room. I ran to the cell where the remaining detainees were being held.

"I need this door open now!" I told the guard as I pushed past him into the room. Crossing to the first prisoner, I lifted his hood. There was no resemblance to Muhammad Ibrahim. The same was true of the second detainee. The third seemed no more promising. The man in the photo I carried was slim and fit. I could see immediately that the last prisoner had a belly that lapped over his belt buckle. But when I lifted the hood, I didn't need to raise it any further than his chin. He had a distinctive dimple. I would have known it anywhere.

"You're Muhammad Ibrahim," I said numbly, without even considering my words. "I've been waiting to meet you."

He said something in Arabic. The guard outside the cell door translated for me. "He says that you are the interrogator in the blue shirt." I later found out that I had gained a reputation in Tikrit for that shirt. Since I wore it practically every day, it made me easily identifiable. There had even been, I was told, a bounty out for the American in the blue shirt.

I was sure that I had the man I'd been hunting for so many weeks. It didn't seem possible that in the end, it would have been as easy as walking into a prison cell and picking him out. But that's how it happened, and in that moment I had a sudden rush of hope. We had tracked up the ladder, through the ranks of street thugs and informants and former bodyguards and insurgent lieutenants. We had penetrated their network to virtually its highest level. We had captured scores of bad guys and maybe saved hundreds of lives in the process. If we could do all that, maybe we could take this last step. Maybe Muhammad Ibrahim really could take us to Saddam.

But first I had to be absolutely certain that this was the man I was after. With so many dead ends and blind alleys, I'd become accustomed to last-minute screwups. I led the prisoner out into the hallway and left him with the guard. Then I dashed back to where Basim and the others were waiting. I grabbed the driver and took him to his cell. Then I signaled for the guard to bring out Muhammad Ibrahim. As he stood in front of the cell door, I raised his hood just high enough for Basim to see what I had seen: that unmistakable chin.

The instant he saw it, Basim leapt up and backed into the corner, as far away from the powerful Hamaya as he could get. He gestured frantically for Muhammad Ibrahim to be taken away. There was a look of stark terror on his face. I gestured to the guard, and when he had taken the prisoner out of sight, I turned to Basim.

"Is that him?" I asked.

Basim just nodded. He was sobbing and muttering under his breath.

John, listening to the driver, smiled. "He thinks you are one bad motherfucker, Eric," he translated.

I looked at Basim, trembling and tear-stained. Our eyes met as he said something else. "You are close," John translated. "You are so close."

"Thank him for me," I replied. "Thank him for his help." I reached out and we shook hands. It was the last time I ever saw Basim Latif.

CHAPTER 18

BANGING ON THE DOOR

0506 13DEC2003

It was just after 0500. The admiral's plane would be leaving at 0800, but Lee and I had been told to be at the flight line at 0700. That gave me two hours to interrogate Muhammad Ibrahim. I may have been in the zone, but this was a man who, I believed, reported directly to Saddam. He would have a lot of secrets to hide and a lot of incentive to hide them. I had my work cut out for me.

I took Basim, Muhammad Khudayr, and the other detainees back to their cells. I wasn't going to use them to convince or manipulate this prisoner into talking. This time it was just going to be Muhammad Ibrahim and me. I would be facing the man I considered to be the second most valuable target in Iraq, and I had one hundred and twenty minutes to find out what he knew. I could go in one of two directions. I could try to work down the link diagram and get the locations of the men who followed his orders, all the brothers and cousins and friends who made up his insurgent network. Or I could move up the last rung of the ladder to the man who gave orders to Muhammad Ibrahim.

I didn't think twice. I'd never have this opportunity again. I was going to swing for the fence.

"My name is Eric," I told the prisoner as we sat face-to-face. "I've been looking for you a long time, Muhammad Ibrahim. I need you to listen to me very carefully. You and I will be talking about just one thing: the exact location of Saddam Hussein."

He looked from me to John and back again. Then he smiled, exposing his tobacco-stained teeth. "I don't know where he is," he said.

"You know exactly where he is. I know you do. That's why I've been looking for you. That's why I've gone after your entire family. That's why I've brought in every one of your friends. I haven't been looking for Saddam. I have been looking for the man who is going to take me to Saddam. That man is you."

"You give me too much credit," he replied, the smile still on his face.

"I'm not the one giving you the credit. Everyone I've talked to gives you the credit. They all say that it's you who's running the insurgency. They tell me that you are a very important person, very well respected and very much feared. It's because of that respect and fear that Saddam picked you to lead his insurgency. They tell me that you were the one that handed out Saddam's money. They tell that you have men in Samarra and Fallujah. They tell me that Radman worked directly for you."

"Where is Radman?" he asked. I knew that he was testing me. He wanted to find out the limits of my information. Would I tell him the truth or try to bluff him?

"Radman is dead," I told him.

He didn't seem surprised. Instead he sat staring at me, waiting to see what I would do next.

"Now that I have you, I'm going to go after the rest of your family," I continued. "I will go after every brother, son, cousin, and nephew you have. You are about to bring down hell on your family and it won't be over until we find Saddam. If you don't tell me where he is, maybe they will. You can stop that right now. Give me Saddam and I stop hunting them."

"I don't believe you," he said contemptuously.

"Look at me and listen carefully. You will give me Saddam. When you do I will allow you to leave here a free man. I will do that because you have given me the most wanted man in the world. When that happens, I will help you. Until that happens, I can't help you. There is only one thing you need to think about and that's how you will be able to go home. I'm the only one who can make that happen."

"Even if I knew where Saddam was and if I took you to him, they would know it. They would kill my family. You could not stop them."

For the first time, the prisoner was giving me a glimpse of what his terms for talking might be. He wanted protection for himself and his family. We had gone from outright denial to conditional cooperation. *If* he knew where Saddam was. *If* he took us to him. That one little word made all the difference.

"Who are 'they,' Muhammad Ibrahim?" I asked. "Who's going to come after you when Saddam is gone? You are running his insurgency. Without you, Saddam has no power. Those men who are loyal to him will see that. They will stop fighting. They will respect and fear you even more because you have brought him down. Listen to me. This country is going to be rebuilt from the ground up. The old regime will never give up as long as Saddam is still out there. When we capture him, with or without your cooperation, they will know that it's all over. They'll give up the struggle. You can go home. Your family will be safe. Iraq will have a new beginning."

As the minutes ticked down, I expanded on the vision of the nation free from Saddam. At regular intervals he would try to interrupt. He couldn't help me, he insisted. He didn't know where Saddam was hiding. But I just kept at it. I hammered home the fear and danger that existed for him, his family and his country if Saddam weren't captured. Then I contrasted it with the safety and security they would enjoy if the dictator were run to ground. I made it as personal as I could. It was a matter of duty, I told him. He had a responsibility to his family and to Iraq. The old rule of terror and intimidation was over. A new world was coming. He could help to make that happen. And in the process he would guarantee the future of the entire Al-Muslit clan.

It was nearly 0645. "If you don't help me, Muhammad," I told him, "I can't help you. The only life your family will ever know is being on the run. They will be fugitives and outlaws. And your country will be torn apart. It's up to you."

If anything I was saying got through, he didn't let me know. He just stared at me without expression. Without an outward sign, I had no idea if he was even close to breaking. But I was surer than ever that, if he wanted to, he could take me to Saddam.

Lee came to the door and silently tapped his wristwatch. It was time to go. "Muhammad," I said, "I am going to put you back into your cell. No one is going to come to talk to you again. You are going to be taken away to spend the rest of your life in a dark prison by yourself. Your family is going to be hunted like animals. Saddam can't help them. No one can help them, except you, right here, right know. Now that we have captured you, you are of no use to Saddam. He will not help you and he won't take care of your family. This is your only chance to help them."

I waited for him to respond. He just glared at me.

"You have one way out," I said, standing up and signaling to John that the interrogation was over. "You know what that way is. When you are back in your cell, think hard. Think about your family. Think about your country. Then, when you change your mind and decide to take me to Saddam, I want you to bang on your cell door. Do it as loud as you can, otherwise I'm not going to hear you. And if I don't hear you, you will never leave that room a free man. Do you understand what I'm telling you?"

"Yes, but—"

"Shut up!" I shouted. "There is only thing I want to hear from you: the location of Saddam. Otherwise, don't say anything." I turned to leave, then stopped and faced him again. "Just bang on the cell door, Muhammad. That's all you have to do."

I left, slamming the wooden door on my way out.

★ ★ ★

At a little before 0700, I found Lee back at the prison.

"I need to get an analyst to let someone know that we had actually caught Muhammad Ibrahim in that raid," I told him. "I also need to give Kelly a call in Tikrit."

"Make it quick," Lee said. "We're supposed to be there already."

I hurried to the TOC—the Tactical Operations Center—and found the only analyst on duty. I gave him as much information as I could, as quickly as possible, then I e-mailed Kelly. He needed to know that we had Muhammad Ibrahim and that, so far, he hadn't given Saddam up. By the time I finished it was 0710. I was running late. Lee was already waiting in a truck outside the prison. It was only then that I realized that I didn't have my gear.

"Lee, I haven't packed yet. Give me a couple of minutes."

"Get in," he said. "I'll drive you over there. We've got to make sure we're on the admiral's plane."

We took off for my tent, raising a cloud of dust behind us. For the first time since I had gotten news of the raid I had a chance to catch my breath. The satisfaction of having finally confronted Muhammad Ibrahim was mixed with the regret of not having gotten him to talk. It would be up to someone else now to finish the job.

"So," Lee said as we bounced along toward the airstrip, "you got your guy."

"Yeah," I replied. "I've been looking for that son-of-a-bitch for three months."

"What did you do to him, Eric?"

I turned to Lee. "What do you mean? I didn't do anything to him."

"Well, something happened. I heard him in there while you were at the TOC. He's beating the shit out of that cell door."

Lee wasn't even done talking by the time I threw open the truck door. "I've got to get back to the prison!" I shouted. "He wants to give it up. Can you hold the plane?"

Lee didn't even blink. "Go!" he said. "Hurry!"

I jumped out. I don't think I realized we were still moving. My boots hit the ground and I tumbled head over heels and in the dirt. I did a combat roll, trying to recover, and leapt to my feet. I looked around, hoping nobody had witnessed my dumb move, and then started sprinting for all I was worth. I raced the quarter mile back to the prison. At the main entrance a guard stopped me. "Hold up," he said. "Where do you think you're going?"

"I'm an interrogator," I told him, trying to catch my breath. "I need to get in there and talk to someone right now."

"Are you cleared to work here?" he asked, looking at me suspiciously.

"Yes," I replied. "I've been with the task force since July." I gave him my name and he started methodically checking through a stack of papers.

"Sorry," he said at last. "I don't see your name here."

"Look," I said, taking a deep breath. "I really don't have time for this . . ."

"I'm not supposed to—"

"I need to get in there, *now!*" I barked. Startled, he waved me through.

I hunted down John in the break room. "Muhammad Ibrahim is banging on the cell door, John," I told him. "You know what that means."

He leapt up and together we ran down the hallway to where a group of guards had gathered outside the prisoner's cell. As we approached, we heard the unmistakable sound of a fist hammering on the door. The noise was deafening.

"I don't know what the hell got into that crazy bastard," one of the guards said as we rushed up. "All of sudden he just started screaming and pounding. We can't get him to shut up. He's been going at it for ten minutes."

"It's okay," I replied. "Let's get him out of here and back into the interrogation room."

A few minutes later Muhammad Ibrahim was sitting in front of me again. I pulled off his hood and saw his angry red eyes.

"Why am I being treated like this?" he demanded. "I have only done what you told me to do."

I nodded, trying to calm him down. "Right," I said. "You banged on the cell door, just like I told you. So where is he? Where is Saddam?"

"I want to talk to Paul Bremer," he said. His whole demeanor had changed. A half hour ago, he was facing the prospect of a lifetime in prison for him and his family. Now suddenly, with the prospect of freedom, he was back in charge. But there was no way I'd be able to get him to the civilian head of the provisional government.

"Listen to me, asshole," I said. "There is no Paul Bremer on this deal. It's just you and me. Who do you think had your family arrested? Who do you think found out about your friends Basim and Abu Drees and Thamir Al-Asi? It was me, the interrogator in the blue shirt. I'm the one you cut the deal with. Paul Bremer doesn't know who you are and doesn't care. I'm the only one who can help you. So let's cut the shit."

"I need this to be official before I say anything," the prisoner said, trying to stare me down. "I need it written out and signed by the commanding general of this post. He is the man I want to talk to. Right now."

"What is your deal?" I asked. "What do you want?"

"I want me and everyone in my family released and protected."

"That's forty people," I replied. "We'd have to know where they are at all times." The negotiation had begun. He was bargaining from a position of strength now. Both of us understood that he had something I wanted. By banging on the cell door he had acknowledged that he knew where Saddam was. We also both understood that he was starting the bartering by making a lot of unreasonable demands to see exactly what he could gain.

"We can all live in the same neighborhood," he said. "Your soldiers can guard us there."

I pretended to think it over. There wasn't a chance any of this was actually going to happen, but I had to keep the process moving forward. "Done," I said finally. "But that's after we get Saddam."

"Then bring me to the general," he countered.

This was getting me nowhere. "Look, Muhammad," I said. "I'm the only one who knows who you really are. No one is going to believe you unless I convince them that you're telling the truth. I'm the one you have to deal with."

"I want to talk to the commanding officer."

We were quickly reaching a dead end. I had to regain the momentum. "Okay," I said. "I'll try to get a senior officer in here."

"He must have authority to sign the agreement," Muhammad Ibrahim insisted. "We must develop a plan." Suddenly he wanted to be in charge of the mission to capture Saddam. He had been an important man for so long he couldn't get used to the idea that he'd be turning over his most valuable piece of information to a guy twenty years his junior. But the bottom line was that he was ready to give it up, and I had to keep him focused on that.

Leaving the prisoner with John and a guard, I rushed down the hallway to the entrance. Lee had come back and was waiting at the guard desk.

"Muhammad Ibrahim is ready to talk," I told him. "But I've got to find someone who's got the authority to sign off on a deal."

"Admiral McCraven is waiting at the flight line," Lee reminded me. "But the J-3 is still around." That would do: the J-3 was the second in command at the base, a colonel.

"Where can I find him?" I asked. "I need a full bird for this."

"He is usually asleep right now," Lee replied. "The guy works twenty-hour days."

"Will he mind if we wake him up?"

"We can try," Lee said with a laugh. "Once he's down, it's hard to get him up. I know. I've tried."

He was right. After shouting in his ear, we were finally able to get the colonel to open his bloodshot eyes. He stared at us confused and still half asleep. "What's going on?" he mumbled.

I explained the situation as clearly and quickly as I could. I could only hope I was reaching him through his haze of fatigue.

"So what do you want me to do?" he asked when I was finished.

"I need you to put on your uniform and sign a document."

The colonel yawned. "Okay," he said. "I'll be over there in a minute." He laid his head back down on the pillow and closed his eyes. I looked at Lee in frustration. He shrugged and tapped his wristwatch again. We left the tent and stood outside for a short, intense conversation.

"Lee," I said. "I've got to get back to prison and get Muhammad Ibrahim ready for the J-3."

He shook his head. "I don't think the colonel is going anywhere," he told me. "I'm not even sure he heard you. Besides, it's 0740. We've got to get out to that plane now."

"But what if we explained all this to the admiral?" I asked urgently. "Do you think he'd stay?"

"I don't think it would do any good. He's on his way to

brief General Abizaid's J-2." He saw the desperate look on my face. "All right," he said. "I'll do the best I can." He looked at his watch. "That flight is going to take off at 0800. Be there."

I took off as fast as I could back to the prison, where Muhammad Ibrahim was waiting with John. I must have sprinted three miles in the last hour.

"There is an officer coming," I told the prisoner. "He'll have the agreement ready to sign. After that, you'll have thirty seconds to tell us what you know. I'm not fucking around with you anymore, Muhammad."

"I will tell him," he assured me.

"What are you going to tell him?"

"That I will help you find Saddam."

"No motherfucker," I shouted. "You're not going to help anything. You are going to do it. You are going to take us there or you are never going anywhere again." It was time to remind him who was really in charge now.

"You want to go?" he shot back. "Let's go. You and me. We will go right now."

"Don't fuck with me. I want the location. The exact location." I had no time to try and arrange another hit. I had to find out where Saddam was hiding and get the information passed along before I left.

"Then I will take you there." He was actually going to give us Saddam. I could see that he was both terrified and excited by the prospect.

"You will take us," I told him, "but not now. You'll go tonight, with the soldiers." By that time, maybe a hit could be set in motion. I leaned in close, inches from his face. "He has to be there," I told him, "or you get nothing."

"He will be there," he replied, staring back at me without blinking.

"Be where?" I pressed. I had to have the location.

He was silent. I could hear the seconds ticking by in my head. If he didn't tell me now, he might never tell anyone. I had pushed him into this corner. It was strictly between him and me. Anyone else would have to start all over again. And by then it might be too late. Saddam might be somewhere, anywhere else. All my experience as an interrogator had come down to this one moment. It had taken me two hours to break one of the most important insurgents in Iraq. If he was going to talk, it had to be before he had a chance to change his mind. It had to be now.

"He is at a farm in Ad Dawr," Muhammad Ibrahim said at last in a low, hoarse whisper as John translated. "It is south of Tikrit, just east of the river."

"Whose farm?"

"It belongs to a man named Qies Niemic Jasim."

I grabbed a sheet of paper and a pencil. "Tell me the location," I said.

I frantically drew a map as he talked, taking down as many details as possible. One of the other interrogators, a guy named Scott, stuck his head in the door. "Lee called from the flight line," he told me. "He said it's time to go. The admiral's waiting."

"I know you don't know who I am," I told Scott. "I realize you have no reason to believe me." I handed him the scrawled paper. "But this is a map of the location of Saddam Hussein. Please call Tikrit and talk to Kelly. He's the analyst there. Tell him Muhammad Ibrahim was captured last night and he is going to take us to Saddam." I turned back to the prisoner and we exchanged a final look. "He has to be there. You have to be right or you'll never see daylight again."

He nodded. "I will take you." He seemed calm now, almost relieved. He had nothing left to hide. And I had found out what I needed to know. We had both reached a turning point.

CHAPTER 19

ACE IN THE HOLE

0810 13DEC2003

Lee was waiting for me at the runway when I pulled up a few minutes later. The huge C-17 that would take us to Doha was revving its engines. The noise reminded me of my time as an infantryman back in the 82nd Airborne Division.

"Did you talk to the admiral?" I shouted as he walked toward the cargo hold.

He nodded, but I could see from his expression that the news wasn't what I'd hoped for. "I don't think he was really paying attention," Lee said. "I told him that you had gotten information that might lead us to Saddam and he just nodded. I don't think I got through to him. Maybe you should try."

I spotted Admiral McCraven making his way up the back ramp of the plane with his entourage of analysts and assistants. I hurried to catch up with him.

"Good to see you, Sergeant Maddox," he said. "Are you ready to give that brief?"

"Yes, sir," I replied. "But I think you should know that the situation has changed. We got Muhammad Ibrahim last night and he's given us a location for Saddam." He stared at me blankly. As the commander of the entire task force in Iraq, he was dealing with a flood of information on a daily basis. If what I was telling him were true, he probably assumed that he would have already heard it from higher up the chain of command. I'm not sure whether he just didn't believe me or decided to wait to get confirmation from a more reliable source. Whatever the case, it wasn't going to interfere with this important trip to Doha. The plane was already taxiing out to the runway. I sat down and strapped myself in. We were leaving Iraq and nothing I could say now was going to change that.

As we lifted off I found myself wondering whether the admiral would want me to include the interrogation of Muhammad Ibrahim in my CENTCOM briefing. I was still wondering two and half hours later when we touched down in Doha. As soon as we stopped rolling, the admiral stood and headed out of the plane. His staff trailed behind, trying to keep up with his long purposeful strides as he walked toward a group of men who had arrived from CENTCOM to meet him.

I rushed to gather up my gear and follow. I wanted another chance to talk to him, but I was slowed down by all my bags and rucksacks that I'd hurriedly packed just before we took off. I had tied it all together with dummy cord and by the time I got onto the runway, stuff was dropping everywhere. A plastic canteen clattered onto the tarmac making a terrible racket. I could hear Lee trying to stifle his laughter behind me.

"Just keep going," he said. "I got it." He followed along, picking up the scattered debris. I really wanted to talk to the admiral, but I had too much luggage hanging and falling off me to make much progress. When I finally caught up with him, the admiral turned to me. "Now tell me again what happened last night, Edward," he said.

"It's Eric, sir," I replied and went on to walk him through Muhammad Ibrahim's capture once more.

This time I caught his attention. "We got Muhammad Ibrahim?" he asked.

"Yes, sir," I replied. "And just before we left he told me that he would take us to Saddam. Sir, he drew a map to the location. They have it back at BIAP."

I could see that the information was finally sinking in. Just then, a CENTCOM representative approached us. He was visibly excited and he told the admiral that he needed to call Tikrit immediately. They quickly headed off toward the terminal.

Ten minutes later Admiral McCraven was back. "Tikrit is very excited about this," he told me. "They're going to try to put something together." He turned to his staff. "We're going back," he told them. "Just as soon as they gas this thing up. There is no way in hell I'm going to be out of Iraq when we bring in the big guy."

My heart started pounding. I was going back to finish what we'd started. Somebody up there liked me. Then admiral looked back at me. "I want you to stay here, Sergeant Maddox," he said. "You need to brief General Custard on the link diagram as we planned."

I looked at Lee in disbelief. If anyone needed to go back, it was me. I needed to see this thing through. My first reaction was to try to talk him into letting us return with him. But I didn't say anything because I knew it wouldn't have done any good. The admiral wasn't asking for my opinion. He'd already decided.

"Wish us luck," the admiral said as he headed back to the flight line.

I swallowed hard but couldn't hold back my feelings. "It wasn't luck, sir," I said. He stopped and looked back, staring at me for a long moment. Then he turned on his heels and strode toward the bird.

The soldier who had been waiting to drive us from the flight line stepped forward and introduced himself. He was Sergeant Peters and he had been listening in on the conversation. "So you know where Saddam is hiding?" he asked with raised eyebrows.

"Yeah," I replied distractedly as I watched the refueling trucks pull up to the plane.

"Is he full of shit?" the sergeant asked Lee.

"Normally, I'd say yes," Lee joked loudly enough for me to hear. "But in this case he just got finished talking to the one guy on the planet who actually knows where Saddam is hiding."

"So why didn't you go back?" Peters asked.

"I guess they don't really need us anymore," I said. It was hard to admit, but it was true. All they had to do now was get Muhammad Ibrahim to lead them to the farm. My work was done. It was up to the rest of the team now.

"Hey," said Sergeant Peters, "the admiral was coming out here for a few days of R&R. I was supposed to drive him around. You guys want to go instead?"

I looked at Lee and shrugged. "Why not? The briefing's not until tomorrow morning. We've got nothing else to do."

Six hours later, I was sitting in my deluxe hotel room with a view of downtown Doha. A wave of exhaustion swept over me. I had been running on pure adrenaline for the last three days. It had finally caught up with me and I could barely keep my eyes open.

We had spent the afternoon getting a quick look around Doha, ending up at a high-end restaurant where Admiral McCraven had a reservation. We had a delicious Middle Eastern meal, the best food I'd eaten in five months. Of course, everything tastes better with cold beer, and Lee and I kept them coming. For the first time since I'd arrived in Iraq, I could feel myself starting to unwind. There is no better feeling than that first meal, that first beer, and that first breath of freedom after a deployment. I couldn't help but think about what might be going on back in Tikrit, but I wasn't going to let it interfere with the good time I was having with my best friend.

★ ★ ★

In the middle of the night I woke up suddenly. The bedside clock read three A.M. With nothing else to do, I turned on the television. By some miracle it was tuned to ESPN. There was an announcement being made that sent a rush of pure joy through me: Jason White, the phenom quarterback for the Sooners, had won the 2003 Heisman Trophy.

It was an amazing capper in what had appeared to be a heartbreaking season for the Sooners. A week ago to the day they had been crushed by Kansas State in the Big Twelve championship game. Back then I was still in Tikrit, hunting down the two Muhammads in Samarra. It seemed like years ago. Life was full of disappointments. A week ago, OU had lost and for all I knew, Saddam had slipped through our fingers again. But there were consolations, too. Jason White had won the Heisman, and the Sooners were still going to the championship game. Anything could happen.

★ ★ ★

At 0700 I was in the lobby with Lee, showered, shaved, and dressed in my most presentable clothes, which were nothing more than a pair of cargo pants and my trusty blue shirt, washed and pressed by the hotel laundry. Sergeant Peters had come to pick us up for the briefing with General Custard.

"Hey," he said casually as we walked to the SUV, "I went back to the office after I dropped you guys off last night."

"Yeah?" I said, only half listening as I went over my mental notes for the briefing.

"Yeah," he replied. "I found out they did a recon with your guy last night."

My head snapped in his direction and I could feel my stomach lurch. "What happened?" I managed to stammer.

"I was watching it on the satellite feed last night. That guy Muhammad Ibrahim showed them a location. There was a guy on the roof and another one walking around the house. They looked like they were pulling guard."

That was exactly what I would have expected at any location where Saddam was hiding. There wouldn't have been a large presence; just a few men pulling guard. But if they had found Saddam last night wouldn't Sergeant Peters have been a little more excited? Had the whole thing gone wrong again?

"What happened?" I repeated, preparing myself for the worst.

He shrugged. "It was getting late," he said. "I went to bed around 1800."

This guy's got to be shitting me, I thought. They were about to raid a location where Saddam might be hiding and he went to bed? The least he could have done was give me a call at the hotel.

I was trying my best to contain myself as we drove through morning traffic to the base. It wasn't easy. As I sat silently in the back of the SUV, I succumbed to a full-blown anxiety attack. I was clutching my pant legs to keep my hands from shaking. At every stoplight I had to restrain myself from jumping out and running to CENTCOM headquarters. I had to know what was happening. Lee was riding shotgun next to Sergeant Peters. He knew what I was going through but there was nothing he could say to calm me down. All I wanted to hear was the answer to one question: did we get him?

We arrived at CENTCOM and followed Sergeant Peters through a maze of crowded hallways. I looked at the faces of everyone we passed, hoping for a clue as to what might have happened last night. We arrived at our destination and he knocked at the door. An Army major stuck his head out and looked us over warily. "Hey, what's up?" Sergeant Peters asked.

"Nothing," the major replied. He looked distracted, as if he wanted to get rid of us and get back to his work.

I think our driver finally realized the excruciating anxiety I was feeling. "Hey, sir," Sergeant Peters persisted, "did anything happen last night?" I appreciated his effort to find out about last night.

"What do you mean?" the major replied.

"Did they get anyone on that raid last night?"

The major craned his head out to see if anyone was within hearing distance. "Yeah," he said in a low whisper. "We got him."

I didn't laugh. I didn't cry. I didn't make a sound. I just stood there. I wasn't thinking about the long months I had spent trying to get to this moment. I wasn't thinking about all the dead ends and frustrating failures. I wasn't even thinking about the team I had worked so closely with or the men like Jeff and Bam Bam and Kelly who had believed in what I was doing. Instead I was thinking about Barry Sanders.

Barry Sanders was the great running back from OSU. Even though he was an Oklahoma State Cowboy, I had always considered him the greatest football player ever. But it wasn't his record of accomplishments that brought him to mind. It was the way he would handle himself after he scored a touchdown. He never danced or dropped to his knees or showboated in any way. He'd simply hand the ball to the referee and jog to the sidelines. Whenever I heard him interviewed he was humble about his achievements, no matter how impressive they were. As I stood in the hallway at 0800 on December 14, 2003, I told myself one thing: Barry Sanders. Remember Barry Sanders.

I don't remember hearing or seeing anything for a few moments. But as my senses slowly returned, I realized that Lee had grabbed me by the arms. "You did it, Eric," he was saying. "Holy shit! You did it."

Sergeant Peters just stared. The major looked confused. "This is the interrogator who got the target for last night," the sergeant explained. The major immediately escorted us into a small office, where he showed us the first photos taken of Saddam. As I stared at the bearded, bewildered man, the major filled us in on the details of the raid.

The team back in Tikrit, along with the other two teams from Baghdad, had conducted the actual hit, while the 4th ID had cordoned off a large area around the farm. The operators searched for the first hour, but found nothing. Muhammad Ibrahim was yelling at Qies Niemic Jasim, the man who lived at the farm, to show them where Saddam was hiding. Muhammad Ibrahim apparently knew the exact spot, but didn't want to be the one to pinpoint it. He wanted Qies to do the deed. Finally Muhammad Ibrahim realized that it was going to be up to him. He moved to an area just meters away from where the team was concentrated, and began inconspicuously kicking the ground. Two of the team members noticed that he was slowly uncovering a length of rope. Muhammad Ibrahim had taken them to the spot, the exact spot. The team dug up the rope to reveal the trapdoor to the spider hole where Black List #1 was crouching. When the trapdoor was opened, the shooter ordered him to hold up his hands. He lifted one, then the other, trading off a Glock pistol between them as he did so. Finally, with the help of a terp, he complied and dropped the pistol. With both arms raised he was yanked out of the hole.

"We never would have found him without that bodyguard," the major concluded.

"What are they going to do with Saddam?" Lee asked.

"They've got him back at BIAP," the major replied, and then turned to me. "I think your brief with General Custard has been cancelled," he said. "But there's a bunch of analysts who want to talk to you."

"Sure," I said. I was beginning to regain my equilibrium. Shock was giving way to exhilaration.

I followed the major through another door and into a large conference room where half a dozen analysts were waiting. As they took their seats, I started in with my now-standard briefing. There was only one difference: it was no longer just a theory. As of that morning, it had been proven right.

"How did you know where to start?" one of the analysts asked after I had finished my presentation.

"I didn't," I replied. "I let the detainees' information guide me from the beginning. Arriving in Tikrit, I didn't know anything. I didn't have any preconceptions. That worked to my advantage. I could create a link diagram based on what I was being told by prisoners, not what others had already assumed."

"What approach worked best for you in interrogating?" another analyst wanted to know.

"Utilizing family members of the actual bad guys," I replied. "A lot of these detainees weren't actual insurgents. But many of them had important information that I needed. I made sure they understood that, as family members of the terrorists, they were deeply involved. It was guilt by association. But I also made sure they knew that, if they were innocent and cooperated, they would be set free. I also used family members to confront each other. That proved very effective. It had a greater impact when a close relative knew you were lying and said so than if I said it. I took advantage of those relationships whenever I could."

"What can Saddam tell us?" the same analyst asked as a follow-up question. News of the capture had been immediately relayed to the intelligence staff of the task force.

"For one thing," I replied, "he can tell us the location of a few billion dollars he has stashed away in Syria and Turkey. That's the money he was going to use to finance the insurgency and rebuild his regime once we left Iraq."

"Will he talk?" another analyst wanted to know.

"He'll talk to me," I replied confidently, but still trying to maintain Barry Sanders humility. "He'll want to know who betrayed him. He'll want to know how he was captured. We can trade on that information."

With that, the session came to an end. The analysts gathered around to congratulate me and a half hour later, Sergeant Peters had dropped us back at the hotel. Our plane home was scheduled for later that night. I spent the rest of the day in a daze. It was clear from watching television that the news had not yet been released. We had both been instructed not to tell anyone what had happened or that we were on our way home. We had no objections. With everything that had gone down in the last twenty-four hours, we were both half expecting to be called back to Iraq anyway.

Instead we boarded a commercial flight to London. I tried to sleep on the long flight, but the process of decompressing had only just begun. I kept having intense dreams, usually involving interrogations. More than once Lee had to wake me up as I shouted out in the crowded cabin.

Shortly after we touched down at Heathrow, the news was finally broken. Saddam Hussein had been captured. As I sat in the airport pub listening to the excited buzz around me, I felt keyed up and bone tired at the same time. I was looking forward to going home. But part of me would always miss the camaraderie I had shared with the team in Iraq. I had come into the war not really knowing what I could do or how I could serve. Now I had no doubt. I was an interrogator. It was as much a part of me as my name, rank, and serial number.

EPILOGUE

Whatever the rest of the world might have thought about the capture of Saddam Hussein, the American military saw it as a milestone in the war.

That much became clear almost as soon as our plane arrived in Washington, D.C. Word had traveled fast and, by the next morning, Lee and I had already been summoned to brief the head of the Defense Intelligence Agency, Admiral Lowell Jacoby. Also present was General Burgess, the Army's Commander of Special Operations.

"Sergeant Maddox, I've heard some remarkable things about you over the past two days." The admiral stood as Lee and I were escorted into his office. "To tell you the truth, the story I got must be exaggerated because it's just so . . ." he paused. "Well, why don't you tell us in your own words?"

When I finished an hour later, none of the top brass in the room said a word. It was Admiral Jacoby who finally broke the silence. "Sergeant Maddox," he began, "as head of the DIA, there's an award I'm allowed to give out. It's called the Director's

Award. It's the highest honor that can be given in the DIA and it's usually handed out to civilians. But I'm permitted to award it to military personnel if the situation presents itself. I think the situation has just presented itself." Then, right there on the spot, he pulled the citation out of his desk drawer and read it aloud. I might have been honored if I'd heard what he read, but I was too stunned to follow a word he said.

"What does your schedule look like this week?" the admiral asked me when the spontaneous ceremony was over. "The SECDEF is going to want to talk to you as soon as possible."

"Yes, sir," I replied, having no idea what or who the hell the SECDEF was.

"That's the secretary of defense, hero," Lee whispered, coming to my rescue.

★ ★ ★

Two days later, when we arrived at the Pentagon office of Secretary of Defense Donald Rumsfeld, we found that the audience had grown to include Deputy Secretary of Defense Paul Wolfowitz and four-star Marine General Peter Pace, who would later be named chairman of the Joint Chiefs of Staff. Admiral Jacoby was also on hand.

The biggest oak desk I had ever seen dominated the secretary's inner office. He was behind it as we entered, his arms folded across his chest, flanked by floor-to-ceiling bookshelves. He had his trademark scowl on his face, but as we approached, he came out from behind the desk to greet us personally.

"Mr. Secretary," said the admiral, "I would like to introduce you to Staff Sergeant Eric Maddox. He is an Army interrogator and has just returned from Iraq."

"Staff Sergeant Maddox," the secretary repeated in a matter-of-fact tone. He squinted at me from behind his rimless glasses, taking my measure. I liked the fact that he was all business. He wasn't there to hand out compliments. He wanted an actual intelligence briefing.

After introducing Lee, Admiral Jacoby continued. "Mr. Secretary, I would like you to hear Staff Sergeant Maddox's brief firsthand." I had been told I'd have twenty minutes to do my thing. I started in immediately, moving at a fast clip through my last five months in Tikrit. I could tell the secretary was keeping up with me, so I didn't worry about slowing down or repeating key pieces of information. At the twenty-minute mark, he was still listening intently, so I continued, bringing the brief to an end after another ten minutes.

"How close are we to getting the final members of the insurgency?" he asked when I was done.

"Sir," I replied. "I think we are very close."

He finally stopped staring me down and looked over to Admiral Jacoby. "Jake, what the hell is he doing here?" he asked. "He has to go back." I realized that he thought I had come back simply to be awarded for my accomplishments.

"Mr. Secretary," the admiral replied, "their tour is up. Sergeant Maddox's last day was the day that Saddam was captured."

"God," he said, now giving Admiral Jacoby the stink eye. "We're that close to finishing this thing and these two are allowed to come home. I need them back out there."

"Yes, Mr. Secretary," the admiral responded.

"Sir," I chimed in. "Our bags are packed and ready to go." For Lee and me, the war was the most natural place to be. We were interrogators. That was the only place where we could do our job.

At that moment, an aide entered and whispered something

to General Pace. "Sir," the general announced to Secretary Rumsfeld. "I've just gotten a report that eleven million dollars was found in a raid on Muhammad Ibrahim's farm."

The secretary looked me straight in the eyes and stood up. The rest of the room fell silent as he began to applaud. It wasn't just the news of the money or even the capture of Saddam. As soon as I had walked into his office, I knew he was sizing me up. What he wanted to determine for himself was what kind of soldier I was. Meeting with his approval was one of the proudest and most meaningful moments of my military career.

☆ ☆ ☆

It turned out that our rounds in Washington were just getting started. Later that day we were taken to the CIA's headquarters in Langley, Virginia, to brief George Tenet, the head of the CIA. Unlike our meeting with Secretary Rumsfeld, the hour I spent at the CIA was more of a courtesy call, a chance for us to get a pat on the back.

It had only been a few days since Saddam had been rolled up, but I was beginning to realize that there were more than a few people who wished it had happened differently. There had been a lot of intelligence personnel from a lot of different agencies who were assigned full-time to find Saddam. And there were many interrogators and human intelligence collectors who had wanted in on the capture. I could understand their attitude, and their suspicion that I had just been in the right place at the right time. It's a very competitive field and professional envy comes with the territory

But George Tenet was a friendly, easygoing man who basically wanted to add his congratulations as a fellow member of the intelligence community. It was only after I'd finished the briefing and he'd left that a member of his staff leaned over to me and asked, "You want a job, Eric?"

"Don't even think about it," Admiral Jacoby interjected.

He was only half kidding, as I quickly found out. "What are your plans, Sergeant Maddox?" Admiral Jacoby asked me on our way back from Langley.

"He needs a job, sir," Lee interjected. "But he'll never ask you for one." No matter where we were or whom we were with, Lee never had an unspoken thought.

"Sir, I'll be getting out of the Army in April," I explained. "I'm thinking of sending in my application to the CIA and the FBI."

"What about the DIA?" he asked.

"Of course, sir," I replied.

"Go home and relax, Sergeant Maddox," he said. "When you're ready to make your next move, all I ask is that you give me the right of first refusal."

"I will, sir." I paused, then asked the question that had been on my mind since that morning. "Sir, Secretary Rumsfeld mentioned something about Lee and me being sent back to Iraq." I turned to look at Lee, wondering if he was thinking the same thing I was.

He was. "Sir," he told Admiral Jacoby, "as Sergeant Maddox told Secretary Rumsfeld this morning, our bags are packed and ready to go."

★ ★ ★

When we got back to the admiral's office another briefing request awaited us. This one was from General Alexander, the head of intelligence for the entire Army. My presentation to him began like all the others, until he interrupted me by pulling out a newspaper clipping from the *New York Times*. "What is this article referring to?" he asked me sternly. I glanced at the headline: "4th ID Gumshoes Track Down Saddam."

I couldn't believe it. It wasn't just that someone else had rushed in so quickly to claim credit for capturing Saddam. It was that the head of Army intelligence was relying on a newspaper for his information. It made me wonder about the bureaucratic infighting that seemed to run rampant among the various agencies and branches of government.

"I'm sorry, sir, but that story is totally wrong," I told General Alexander. "The media was not allowed anywhere near our operations. Whenever we got a big catch in Tikrit, we would turn it over to the 4th ID. They would brief the press. But no one in the 4th ID had anything to do with getting Saddam."

Maybe I was too direct in my explanation of the 4th ID's lack of involvement. No doubt a three-star general wouldn't be overly impressed by a staff sergeant's opinion. But I was telling him the simple truth; maybe not enough soldiers were asked— or most likely even allowed—to come back and talk honestly about the situation in Iraq.

If I kept my mouth shut, nothing was going to change. But as it turned out, the military actually was interested in what I had achieved and how I did it. Shortly after the whirlwind stop in Washington, D.C., Lee and I received word that General Alexander was sending us on a tour to give intelligence briefings of our time in Iraq. For the next three months we visited bases around the United States, as well as overseas, sharing what we had learned and accomplished in Iraq.

One of our stops was in Fort Bragg, North Carolina, where

I ran into an old friend: Kelly had returned from Iraq and was back at the base. I was happy to see him but didn't really know what to say. So much had happened since we'd last been together, five days before the capture of Saddam. In spite of all the publicity and news coverage, we were still the only two people who knew what had really gone down.

"I've got a souvenir for you, Eric," he said after we greeted each other.

"Is it my share of the 1.9 million?" I asked.

He laughed. "No. We already spent that. But when we pulled Saddam out of the hole we found a couple of things he kept close to him. There was a nine-millimeter pistol that we gave to President Bush. And there was a box of Cuban cigars." He pulled out a cigar and handed it to me. "We saved one for you."

It was one of the nicest gifts I'd ever received. It meant almost as much to me as when, shortly afterward, at my DIA office in the States, I was awarded the Legion of Merit, for actions deemed "pivotal in the extrication of actionable intelligence from numerous detainees which led to the successful detention of various Iraqi former regime leaders and the capture of Saddam Hussein."

★ ★ ★

One of our final stops was Fort Hood, Texas, the home of the 4th ID. As Lee and I drove onto the base the first thing we saw was a huge billboard that showed a hand grasping the Ace of Spades card. Lee and I just stared at each other and I asked him, "Do you think they have any idea what our briefing is about?"

As much as others might try to claim credit for Saddam's

capture, I will always consider it a team effort. Without the confidence, inspiration, and sheer determination shown by the best soldiers in the world, this historic mission would never have been accomplished. I would subsequently receive the National Intelligence Medal of Achievement for my part in the event. It read in part: "Through his professionalism and dedication, Staff Sergeant Maddox developed a unique, comprehensive understanding of the complex networks supporting the former Iraqi leadership. . . . This resulted in the development of actionable intelligence that was provided to analysts and operators and directly resulted in the capture of Saddam Hussein and other senior Iraqi leaders. Staff Sergeant Maddox's distinguished accomplishments reflect great credit upon himself, the United States Army and the Intelligence Community."

That credit, and the pride I feel in those words, also belong to the men with whom it was my privilege to serve.

ACKNOWLEDGMENTS

For their dedicated service and professionalism (and for keeping me alive), I would like to express my sincere gratitude to all the non-commissioned officers with whom I served throughout my military career, specifically Marine Master Sergeant Lee Trevino and Army Staff Sergeant Clif Smith, who have been with me through thick and thin. I also want to thank my family and friends for the unconditional love and support they have always given me, especially my parents, whom I admire so much.

   I would like to thank fellow Oklahoman Bruce Roach, who shared my enthusiasm for this book and whose vision, commitment, and efforts were instrumental in achieving its ultimate publication; Davin Seay for his ability to breathe life into my original, complex manuscript through his amazing writing skills; my agent, William Clark, for dragging me through the streets of New York City to get this book sold; and Jennifer Barth of HarperCollins for believing in me and my story.

Most important of all are my two sons. I am sorry I missed so much of your lives since these wars began. You are my world and I will serve you now.

Eric Maddox

ABOUT THE AUTHORS

Army Staff Sergeant Eric Maddox was awarded the DIA Director's Award, the Legion of Merit, the Bronze Star, and the National Intelligence Medal of Achievement for his key role in the capture of Saddam Hussein. A native of Oklahoma, he now lives in San Antonio, Texas.

Davin Seay has coauthored numerous books, including, most recently, *Hello Charlie*, with Charles Hess; and *In Justice*, with David Iglesias. He lives in Los Angeles, California.